UNDERSTANDING
& HANDLING
DOG AGGRESSION

UNDERSTANDING & HANDLING
DOG AGGRESSION

Barbara Sykes

THE CROWOOD PRESS

CONTENTS

INTRODUCTION

This book deals with aggression and how to establish a foundation of good manners in a dog. Good manners should not be confused with training. It is difficult to train an aggressive dog and can be demoralizing when you feel that you are not succeeding; but educating a dog to have good manners is essential, comes before training and establishes who is pack leader. It is not always easy to digest what an instructor is saying to you when your dog is misbehaving and so the following pages are to help you to have a better understanding of aggression – in your own time and at your own pace.

No two dogs are alike, so it is essential that you study your dog as an individual thus enabling you to understand his learning capacity and to recognise his problem. Never try to run before you can walk and never confront a dog because you invariably will end up as the loser. I do not usually describe case histories but I feel that in the case of aggression it is helpful as it helps to show the great difference in dogs' attitudes, regardless of size or breed.

The only references to breeds in this book are to depict examples of size and character and there is no intention to show that any one breed is more or less aggressive than another. The cover dog is not to be seen as depicting his breed as an aggressive one. He was a rescue brought to me for rehabilitation and so it was far easier to record the progress of a 'resident' dog throughout to help you to understand how he came to be aggressive and how I handled him and his problems. Craig's photograph on the cover shows him as he was, but you will see a far nicer Craig at the end of the book.

There are no tricks or treats in the book; it is about aggression and I make no apologies for writing it as it is. I do not believe in wrapping a nasty tasting sweet up in attractive paper to make it more palatable. Aggression is a serious problem, usually instigated by humans, albeit unwittingly. It is important to reclaim the leadership of the pack and to demote the dog to a pack member: if this means admitting that we have made some mistakes along the way, then so be it, we are only human. The first priority is to sort the problem out and not to lay blame, feel defeated or think that you do not have the magical power others seem to have with difficult dogs. There is nothing special about understanding a dog's mind, we are all capable of doing it, but we have to be willing to see the dog as a dog, realise it has its own form of communication and its own canine instinct. We need to learn how to handle those instincts, not to fight them.

CHAPTER 1

WHAT IS AGGRESSION?

The word 'aggression' produces different responses from different people. It does not necessarily need to have been applied to a dog, since aggression is in evidence in every living being and manifests itself in different ways. When used in connection with a dog it often produces nervousness or even fear. We can accept 'aggression' in human beings but often fail to see anything but harmful behaviour from a dog classed as aggressive. Yet many dogs are often trying only to protect themselves because they have, albeit unwittingly, been put in a position of leadership by their owners and are not mature or experienced enough to handle it correctly.

If human beings are aggressive we do not immediately picture them as attacking everyone they see; at some stage of their lives we may hope that they will have been taught how to handle any aggressive tendencies they may have and how to deal with anger. If they have not received such education, usually from one or both parents when they are young, then it is possible that their aggression will manifest itself violently and often against another human being. However, correct guidance will help a child or a young person to control his or her aggression and in many cases this will provide the encouragement to redirect this energy into becoming a useful tool, not only for themselves but also to help others.

How can aggression be useful and how can it help one's fellow beings? If we think of aggression by using another word we can begin to lose some of the preconceived notions of how it will manifest itself; so let us for the moment forget 'aggression' and replace it with 'indomitable spirit'. Now it is easier to understand how this can be both useful and helpful. It is indomitable spirit that keeps the body going against all odds. When fellow humans are suffering through no fault of their own, as in an avalanche, rock fall, shipwreck, or fire, it is the stubborn, 'never-give-up' spirit of those people in the rescue bid, using their aggression to combat the elements to bring hope to the stranded.

So are 'indomitable spirit' and 'aggression' the same? No, but each one is a product of correct or incorrect channelling of certain characteristics as they show themselves in the human being or the young animal. If a child discovers that, by bullying other children, he not only gets his own way but also experiences what could be termed the 'feel-good factor' he will continue to keep up this behaviour and, if not re-educated, may become aggressive. However, with sensible adult guidance the child's behaviour may be redirected into more acceptable forms, for example, competitive sport, then the aggression can begin to work favourably, and, of course, this would be looked on as admirable and not as something harmful.

Appearances may be deceptive and can cause us to judge without any valid reason. A tall, well-built person is often expected to be strong and capable, but a smaller, more delicate-looking one may appear as needing protection. But time spent with these people may prove that the taller person is quite sensitive and the smaller one well capable

Appearances may be deceptive; large dogs are often thought to be dominant or aggressive but they are just dogs, many of them are big softies. However someone approaching a dog and thinking that it may be aggressive will transmit his or her nervousness to the dog and this may cause it to react in a defensive manner. The relaxed body language of this dog poses no threat but he is still entitled to his own space.

This dog's body is showing signs of tension, the head is dropped and a clear message is being sent that he does not want anyone to enter his space. A dog that is nervous and feels he needs to defend himself may resort to aggression, whereas allowing him to keep his personal space can help him to relax a little.

of looking after him or herself. We are often guilty of judging without any reason other than appearance, and to make a judgement on first sight may cause unnecessary hurt to the individual. This is not to be confused with a person's 'gut instinct': there are times when two people meet and they instinctively like or dislike each other. This is a natural, animal instinct and one that human beings do not always have enough respect for, either in themselves or their dogs. Dogs, like us, have a natural protective 'space' around themselves and they often instantly like or dislike an intruder in that space, it may be another dog or it may be a human. This 'opinion' will not have been made on just an outside appearance, there will be other factors causing the gut instinct to manifest itself. It could be smell, body language, attitude or any other of a number of possibilities; but the dog will not make a judgement, it will simply protect its space. Humans, however, do judge and if they are basing this on appearance rather than knowledge or instinct they may often judge in error, and, to make matters more confusing, they will often bear a grudge too.

If we study human reactions and then compare how a dog would react in similar circumstances it may make it easier to understand. If a human being has a dislike of a fellow being, it may be the result of an instant judgement, a gut instinct or a private feud. They will not want to be in each other's company. Should they know that this is inevitable they will become tense at the thought of meeting; they may even begin to anticipate how the situation will evolve. In fact, if care is not taken, what could have been a sensible, adult conversation between two people who have to be in each other's company for a time may change into an argument whereby little of sense or value is derived from either of them. But the situation can be changed if the people involved control their emotions, curb any aggressive tendencies and either dismiss the meeting from their minds until nearer the time (preventing a build up of negative thoughts) or try to look forward to something

positive about the outcome. The point to bear in mind is that they are forewarned, therefore they can control the outcome if they wish. Knowing the meeting is going to take place means that they can either let aggression dominate their feelings and make the meeting non-productive, or they can be sensitive to each other's feelings, tread with caution and turn what could be a potentially aggressive encounter into something more positive.

Animals are not naturally forewarned other than by sight or smell, and so when they see a person they do not wish to be near they do not take that thought away with them nor do they harbour aggressive feelings towards him. But the next meeting can bring about the same feeling of dislike, partly from memory and partly because the basic instinct is still telling the animal to protect its space. But it will be a short-lived reaction: out of sight out of mind, until smell, action or sight triggers a memory. However, dogs are not relying purely on their own reactions, for if they show a dislike of someone or of another dog then their owner will show a reaction. Then an expected meeting with the dog's current 'enemy' will find the handler conveying his fearful thoughts of the possible outcome to his dog, causing it too to become fearful. This fear may then manifest as nerves, aggression, nervous aggression, or a gleeful anticipation of an event to come that is making its owner exude an air of tension and stress.

A dog would meet a 'threat', deal with it and then get on with its life. If it were to meet the threat again it would act in a similar way; but dogs in their natural environment would fight for survival, they would not deliberately provoke a threat. Dogs are instinctively pack animals, so in their natural world they would have the support and safety of a pack around them and a strong pack leader to guide them. If their human pack leader is conveying the wrong messages or if he is not credible as a strong pack leader then the dog must make its own decisions. If it is not given the freedom to avoid the space of the approaching threat then it will have to defend its own space and this will be with a show of aggression. Whether nervous or dominant, the dog has made the decision and now it will be wary regarding the threat in future, and it will also have lost any respect for its owner as a pack leader.

At this stage you will be able to see how the natural instincts of the dog would make it react to certain situations and how human reactions can affect the dog's attitude. The owner's thoughts transmitted via body language to the dog influence how it deals with a possible threat and can also cause it to harbour a resentment regarding that threat which will surface each time they meet. There is a subtle difference between a dog protecting its space, which is natural if its pack leader does not protect it, and a dog taking a potentially hostile attitude towards a threat because its unsuspecting handler has forced it into a confrontation.

CAN A DOG BE BORN AGGRESSIVE?

There are several reasons why a dog may become aggressive and quite often the problem has been brewing for some time before it is recognised. There are some cases when the aggression is due to breeding, for if a dog with aggression in its genes is bred to another line of aggression then the chances are that at least one, and quite often more, of the young will have aggressive tendencies. Even then it does not have to surface since with correct and sympathetic handling the dog can be educated to subdue its aggression in favour of respect. It is important for all dogs to see their owner as the pack leader, but it is vital that a dog with a dominant attitude and leaning towards aggression not only recognises this leadership but also respects it. It is rare for a dog to be bred so incorrectly that it is beyond redemption and when this does occur it is still down to human error, either through careless breeding or insufficient knowledge of the breed lines being used.

A dog carrying a strong and dominant genetic line can be educated to be a valuable pack member by its handler in much the same way as a sensitive dog can be made either strong or nervous by correct or incorrect handling. If a young dog is sensitive, a potential owner could see it as an attribute, but if a dog is dominant it may be assumed that it could cause problems at a later date. One characteristic is readily acceptable and the other is considered unfavourable yet both are a valuable part of the dog's character; they just need to be balanced. Everything connected with breeding, training and understanding a dog has to be balanced, and, if the scales are kept as even as possible, the youngster will grow to be a well-adjusted, well-balanced dog. However, if the breeder has not understood the genetics of the dog and has not done a very good job of balancing the breed lines, then balancing must be done after the pups have been born. This is rarely a task undertaken by the breeder since the puppies will have gone to new homes long before they reach adolescence (the age when problems begin to materialise). Also due to the very fact that the breeding has not been done with due care, owing to insufficient knowledge by the breeder, it could even be possible that the youngsters have already enjoyed misusing some of their instincts through unsupervised interaction. So the job of balancing the scales will now rest entirely on the new owner, which may seem an onerous task. However, if the dog is handled sympathetically and, given the correct messages from its owner – the new pack leader – in the early stages, the young dog should reach and enjoy adolescence with hardly any problems.

WHAT ELSE CAUSES AGGRESSION?

The saying goes that there is no such thing as a bad dog, only bad handlers. I agree in part, for a dog is rarely naturally bad, it is usually human influence that causes aggression, but

Small dogs appear cute and harmless; they rarely make people feel nervous, which puts people's body language at ease, thus transmitting a calm language to the dog. Here the head is relaxed, the body is at ease and the ears are in a gentle position.

But a dog is a dog and just as large dogs may crave a cuddle, so small dogs are capable of being aggressive. In this picture the body has changed, the dog is leaning slightly back to make it easy to propel itself forwards, the head is turned, the ears are erect and the eyes are focusing. He is clearly not happy about something or someone. A small dog may not get the same reaction from a human as a large dog but they still deserve the same respect.

it does put rather an unkind burden on many handlers since they are not intentionally failing their dog. If a handler refuses guidance or is inconsiderate of his dog's needs, then yes – he is failing the dog. But if a handler in trying to communicate with his four-legged friend is using the wrong language, then he can hardly be considered a bad owner; all that is needed is a common form of communication. Body language can send the wrong messages to a dog, causing it to react in the opposite manner to the one desired by the handler. Correct body language can give a dog a feeling of security; incorrect body language can cause a dog to be nervous.

Many puppies are given toys to play with, the intention being to keep them occupied, to prevent them from being destructive and encourage interaction with their owner. Used correctly and sparingly, puppies can benefit from toys; used incorrectly toys can cause destruction and even aggression.

Other dogs may cause aggression; if a young dog is not getting the security it needs from its owner it may feel threatened by the appearance of an approaching, unknown dog.

Children may make a dog feel insecure, and this can lead to protective aggression, as can strangers in the home, sudden unexpected noises and people running. What appear to be simple games, such as chasing, playing with balls or any form of play that encourages the dog to use its teeth, can cause the dormant aggressive instinct to rise to the surface. This does not mean that games cannot be played nor that other dogs, children and visitors must be avoided, but it does mean that there is an onus on the handler to provide the dog with security, good manners and a dependable pack leader.

If a dog enters a home as an older dog or a rescue dog and is showing aggressive tendencies, it will not always be possible to pinpoint the cause, although most dogs will begin to 'tell' their owner of their past by simple actions. If a dog cowers or snarls at a sudden movement, a clenched fist or a shuffled boot, then it has obviously received treatment from a human that has caused it to be either defensive or defiant and aggressive. In some instances a dog may seem to be quite passive before suddenly bursting into a show of great defiance that may leave its owner baffled. But to the dog, the smell of after-shave, perfume or even oil or grease can kindle an unhappy memory that triggers a show of aggression.

IS AGGRESSION ACCEPTABLE TOWARD A TOY?

No form of aggression is acceptable but many dogs are allowed, and some are even encouraged, to play in a manner that, to the dog, is the foundation training for aggression. It is not going to cause an immediate problem if a puppy shows aggression toward a toy, but as the puppy develops so will his instinct and if the instinct to use his teeth has been nurtured then he will continue to practise this skill. Each time he 'kills' a toy he will gain confidence in his pack skills of hunting, killing and retrieving, and, as all good hunters know, the 'game' must get bigger each time.

Aggression manifests itself in many different ways and it is not peculiar to any specific breed of dog nor to any size. Big dogs are often assumed to be more aggressive than little ones and there can be no argument that if a big dog bites then it can do a lot of damage. But there are many little dogs who look as if butter wouldn't melt in their mouths and have a temper that is not only aggressive but will often flare up with little provocation. Just because a dog is small does not mean its short temper can be dismissed as unimportant, for although not as strong as a larger dog its teeth will be extremely sharp. Inside every small dog is an instinct to defend and be aggressive to obtain security, just as inside every large dog is the desire for affection. It is how we react to these instincts when they first show themselves that determines the final outcome in the adult dog, for if we fail to recognise them in their embryo stages they

Respecting a dog's personal space is important for the safety of both dog and human. This dog is behind a fence and is making it clear he does not want anyone to get any closer.

Here we see how the dog has been pushed into being aggressive. In his mind he is protecting himself and the boundary fence, but having taken just one step closer we can see the change in him. Imagine what would have happened if there had been no barrier. Ignoring a dog's space and his warning signs can end up with serious injury and a dog losing his life.

will become a natural and progressive part of our dog's life. When a dog reaches adolescence it will have learned many things about itself, regardless of what we think it may have learned, for its own natural instincts will have been forming as it has developed. If the scales of learning have been tipped unfavourably toward undesirable tendencies they will need to be balanced again before the dog turns a natural instinct into a bad habit.

Throughout these pages we are not looking at certain breeds or sizes of dogs, we are looking purely and simply at an instinct that on many occasions has helped both humans and animals to survive. We are going to see how it can develop, how it can be prevented, how it can be made to work for us and how we can learn to be a pack leader a dog can be proud to be with. We are going to make friends with aggression.

Who Is the Dog on the Cover?

Craig came to me when he was almost two years old; he was the culmination of all the possible scenarios that can cause aggression rolled into one very frustrated, furious and aggressive dog. His breeding left much to be desired, for although his ancestors were all good dogs far too much inbreeding was prevalent in his line. He had been bought as a puppy by a couple in their early sixties who had never owned a dog before. High-energy food had made him hyperactive and the continuous use of his teeth on his abundance of toys had produced a sense of power that he began using on his owners. These problems, combined with pulling on the lead and no recall meant Craig was in full control. He began being not

only aggressive to other dogs and people but also to his owners. Craig was an example of what may happen if a dog is not given mental and physical boundaries. A dog allowed to be his own pack leader will make decisions that are not acceptable to human beings; insubordination may manifest itself as bad manners, nervousness or aggression. The breed of dog does not necessarily denote how it will show itself so much as the catalogue of events leading up to its believing it can take control. A very small dog may suffer from dominant aggression and a very large dog from nervous aggression. Throughout this book we are going to watch Craig's progress and how he turned from being a problem into a pal.

CHAPTER SUMMARY

A dog will often react to the body language of a human being and may see a tense or stiff body as a show of aggression. This may trigger a reciprocal show of aggression from the dog.

If a dog is allowed to be destructive with toys it may stimulate a dominant instinct.

Both nervous aggression and dominant aggression are the result of a dog making its own decisions, because it has become its own pack leader.

If a dog does not see its owner as pack leader it will automatically assume the leadership.

CHAPTER 2

RECOGNISING AGGRESSION

To recognise aggression may not sound difficult: to recognise it will sound far easier and less complicated than to make friends with it. After all, a dog raises its top lip, snarls and growls, then attempts to bite you, this is undoubtedly aggressive behaviour and who on earth would try or even want to make friends with that? But then if a dog does show such aggressive behaviour the options available to you may be limited. For if you turn and run the dog may chase you; if you stand still it may leap at you; and if you walk towards it there is every chance that it will believe you are challenging it. Any of these options could result in an aggressive attack. But if you were able to recognise the reason for the show of aggression you would have a better understanding of how to react to it, and, yes, in some cases you can actually befriend the aggressor. If you can understand the reason for the dog's behaviour and you can recognise what type of aggression it is feeling then you will be able to create an empathy with it. Not understanding a dog's aggression may cause an accident, but understanding it means that you can sympathise with the animal's needs: whether it needs to feel protected, to be in control, is feeling frightened, wishes to frighten or if it is governed by anger.

Now we have to look a little further at how we can actually judge whether a dog *is* aggressive or whether we *think* it is aggressive, for the wrong decision may actually cause a dog to react in an unfavourable manner when its original intentions may have been quite harmless. For example, some dogs are wonderful at mimicry and when their owners smile at them they will return this show of affection with a curling of the top lip in a reciprocal 'grin'. This same dog can then meet someone who appears to be friendly and it will 'grin' a welcome to him, but if he is not familiar with this expression he may assume that the dog is showing aggression to him. The human reaction then would be to stiffen the body in a nervous or fearful manner; this would alarm the dog which up until this point had only friendly intentions. However, if this person, whom the dog was prepared to be friendly with, is showing aggression (and this is how the dog will see it) then it could reciprocate with a stiffening of its body and maybe even a growl. Now a chain of events will have begun that will have an unhappy ending if the human being does not manage to convince the dog that he is not an aggressor.

READING THE EYES

A dog's eyes will tell you more about its character, feelings and intentions than a curled lip will ever tell you. It may not always be easy to see the eyes (to be so close may mean that you are within the flight or fight distance) and it is never wise to stare into a dog's eyes. To stare at a dog can be an intrusion of its privacy and

It's lovely to see a happy dog rolling on its back for pleasure, often having a good back scratch on the grass and receiving a tummy tickle. But not all dogs are as relaxed and some have an ulterior motive.

security and also be confrontational, but it is possible to get the general picture of a dog's expression without fixing on one feature.

If a dog is aggressive everything about its stance will tell you its intentions; after all, if we approach another human being we can usually tell what kind of a reception we can expect. We automatically 'read' the body language of others; for example, when approaching a total stranger we know instinctively whether he is going to ignore us, has not even seen us, is apprehensive about our approach or appears as if he is going to make conversation. How do we know all this? By 'reading' the body language of this person, and if we get closer and can see his facial expression clearly then we can 'read' even more. A totally blank expression, almost as if we did not exist, would warn us not to make conversation and preferably not even to acknowledge him. A slightly hesitant smile is almost asking us whether we

want to make contact but is not being intrusive. A deliberate attempt to turn away may mean 'I don't want to acknowledge you' or 'I don't know how to acknowledge you.' A warm and friendly smile will be reflected in the eyes and will usually earn an acknowledgement if not exactly a reciprocal greeting. But a smile with the lips when the eyes have a cold, hard expression is worthless and, instead of making us feel at ease, will create a feeling of nervousness and mistrust or even one of dislike.

When we look at the body language of human beings and how we can 'read' their intentions it really is not very hard to 'read' a dog's intentions. In many ways dogs do not differ greatly from us, but, unfortunately, we humans tend to try to make them like us in some ways and then fail to recognise the similarities in others. We are happy to humanise them with beds, toys, balls, towels, jackets and grooming, for instance, but often fail to give them the respect we would give to another human who was a total stranger. We will stare at them, pat them, walk close to them, stand in front of them and even try to cuddle them, yet not have been introduced to them.

Two strangers meeting will not be over-familiar with each other, they will introduce themselves, make polite conversation and quite often will also be discreetly (or in some cases blatantly) taking in each other's general appearance. Two dogs meeting will act in a similar manner, although not necessarily in the same order, they will keep a distance from each other while 'checking out' each other's general appearance. If sight, smell and body language meet with approval then they will start their 'polite conversation'. This, of course, is conducted mainly by nose and is not recognised human behaviour. However, if the dogs do not approve of each other at first sight the scene would be different. If they have plenty of space between them (and the more space there is the more time they have to assess their options) they will make a decision about whether to stay and fight or turn and take flight, hence the term 'fight and flight distance'. If both dogs are of an aggressive nature they could choose to fight; if both dogs are passive and the distance between them is great then they can choose to walk away, but they will be apprehensive of each other until an even greater distance is between them. But if one dog is more aggressive than the other and the distance is within the fight distance (and the aggressor can keep shortening this), then the less aggressive dog would be prudent to become submissive.

Knowledge of eye contact is important since when dogs meet they will use eye contact and this will hold the attention of the one to the other while their bodies begin a conversation. Within the fight distance a dog cannot afford to lose eye contact or it will lose control of the situation. If we think of a sheepdog facing one sheep or of a dog stalking and finally facing a cat the dog in each case is the hunter, the aggressor, and the sheep or the cat is the prey. The dog will hypnotise its prey until it is ready to pounce or, in the case of the sheep, is ready to give in and turn away. But in either case if the hunter loses concentration and averts its hypnotic stare then the prey will see this lapse as weakness and will make its escape. In either case it is instinctive for the prey to run rather than take a stand, but the act of running may often incite the hunter into an attack. It now becomes clear why human eye contact with a dog may be dangerous: to engage in a hypnotic stare with a dog showing dominant aggression may incite the dog into attacking. The same stare with a dog showing nervous aggression could undermine the dog's confidence in human beings even further. Always avoid a confrontation whenever possible.

In the case of two dogs staring at each other within the fight distance, they will circle each other with their bodies stiff and stilted movements until one of them loses concentration for a split second, allowing the other to attack. In the case of neither dog losing its concentration and the distance between them being too close to allow flight, the attack will be simultaneous and fierce.

Having seen how dogs behave and how they expect each other to behave we can see how human behaviour and body language can confuse a dog, thus causing an unwelcome reaction. A dog's eyes are very expressive and if the animal is acting aggressively its eyes will appear cold and hard. A stranger may be looking at a dog absentmindedly or while talking to the dog's owner, but when the dog does not know the person it may see him or her as a threat, and particularly if the stranger's eyes are not reflecting a welcome greeting. The dog will make decisions by using its senses. Its sense of smell will inform it whether the stranger has dogs; this may make it relax or have an adverse reaction according to how confident the dog is with its own kind. Its sight will inform it whether the stranger's body is friendly or aggressive, and, if by this time the stranger is apprehensive about the dog's reaction, there will be a stiffening of the human's body

This dog's body is tense and she is showing signs of nervousness and a degree of fear.

Her lip licking demonstrates how stressed she is. Bending over a dog when it is submissive will only increase its fear, but dogs are resilient and this submissive position will give a dog an opportunity to protect itself with a bite. The dog on top in a fight isn't always in the better position, as it leaves its throat and under carriage exposed to the lower dog's jaw. Always allow a nervous or submissive dog to get up before trying to make contact with it, if not the dog can become more fearful, or aggressive.

If two dogs approach each other for the first-time face to face it can be very daunting, and not something they would instinctively do unless they were prepared to fight if they didn't like each other. Note how the older dog, although taller, is pulling his head back a little, showing uncertainty with no dominance. The younger dog is smaller but stockier and is pushing forwards. These are two well-mannered dogs but imagine how this could go if the younger dog was aggressive.

that can create an aggressive appearance. Or the dog may rely on its owner as a responsible pack leader to protect it by making decisions for it and, in so doing, taking command of any situation which may arise from the meeting. In many cases whatever decision a dog makes can cause problems: jumping up at people, being aggressive or being nervous, but in all cases if the owner is a strong pack leader the dog will leave decision making to him.

We now have three major elements to take into consideration when dealing with aggression: how strong the owner is as a pack leader; the reaction of the third party (dog or human); and the type of aggression.

NERVOUS AGGRESSION

Aggression born of nerves is usually caused by insecurity; it may have been evident when

the dog was young or it may have developed owing to an incident in the dog's life that has left it feeling the need to protect itself. This kind of aggression is not dominant, and dogs with nervous aggression are rarely nasty dogs; they are protecting themselves because they have been put into that position. In some cases the dog may have been a quiet puppy and the owner may have overprotected it, causing it to be nervous of everyday things it may meet such as other dogs, cars, washing machines and people, to name but a few. But a dog can become nervous when the owner fails to give it protection. A classic example may occur when a dog taken out for a walk is attacked by another dog; no matter how the owner of the first dog tried to avoid the situation nor how sorry he was that it happened, in the dog's eyes its owner let it down and therefore can no longer be relied upon for protection. So it now

When approaching each other on an angle their body language is very different. The older dog is more relaxed and the younger one is not pushing forwards. If we want dogs to meet each other and get on together we need to take every precaution. The younger dog is on a loose lead for added security, a tight lead would make him want to pull forwards.

begins growling nervously when it sees other dogs: not because it wants to fight but because it is afraid that it will be attacked. It may seem a hard fact to face that the dog has lost faith in its owner but we have to understand how the dog sees the situation and not how we see it. It is a pack animal and it needs a strong protective leader, so that if he, the leader, shows any sign of weakness in being able to protect his pack then he loses credibility. This means that the dog must rely on itself to handle any situations that may mean a possible threat. A dog with nervous aggression is only a problem because it feels insecure; it is not being aggressive for the thrill of a confrontation, rather it is desperately trying to avoid a confrontation by trying to persuade the 'threat' to leave it alone.

DOMINANT AGGRESSION

A dog with dominant aggression is arrogant and defiant; it firmly believes that it is in control and has a right to make decisions. These decisions invariably lead to a direct confrontation with whatever it is the dog objects to, human or canine. Unfortunately, this kind of dog is not looking for security as it believes it is capable of handling any situation it is faced with and the more it succeeds in being aggressive the more it will be so. This usually causes an unhappy sequence of events for the owner of such a dog, for it is succeeding in getting its own way by being aggressive, which means that the owner is not fully in control of it. When the owner is not in control he will become nervous when he thinks that his dog is going to show aggression to someone or another dog: there will be an instinctive tightening of the body and a change of tone in the voice and the dog will immediately pick up the message that the owner is insecure. It is an interesting observation that aggressive owners can make a dominant dog worse and make a nervous dog develop nervous aggression. A nervous owner will exacerbate nervous aggression in a nervous dog and cause a dominant dog to be aggressive, and a dominant dog can make an owner show nervous aggression.

PROTECTIVE AGGRESSION

This is a totally different type of aggression for, although it can be argued that either a dominant or a nervous dog is protecting either itself or its owner, both these types of aggression are displayed on other occasions. Protective aggression is not as common and is displayed only when the dog feels that it has no alternative but to be protective. It may be protecting itself against another dog, a human family member it believes to be under threat or a canine relative or offspring. However, in most cases a dog will always be prepared to protect itself and defend its pack, human or canine, so that it is in the best interests of the owner to make sure that his dog is never put into that position unless it is absolutely unavoidable. A dog having to protect its pack or its canine young means that its leader is either unavailable or is not strong enough to offer protection; in the case of the latter it could lead to a normally placid dog feeling that its leader is not as strong as he first appeared and therefore developing a more regular show of aggression. A sympathetic approach must always be used when dealing with a dog that is being protective, for if the dog is assuming a role it does not need to take it may have aggressive consequences in the future. But if the dog is genuinely acting in a protective way it needs reassurance without excessive praise; this will be covered in greater detail when we deal with how to handle aggression.

PHYSICAL SIGNS OF AGGRESSION

Just as we need to be able to identify the different kinds of aggression so we also need to be able to physically recognise them. It is not

This picture has so many conversations. Two friends inspecting a new comer, who knows he is out numbered so he drops to a lower position, not showing either dominance or submission. He has judged the body language of the other two dogs wisely, they are not dominant so he is not in danger but if he is too forward they could turn against him. By being cautious and polite he was accepted by them.

difficult to determine that a dog is being aggressive, but quite often by the time we have read the messages of aggression it is too late to avert it or we have too little time to be able to ascertain what kind we are dealing with. Hostility in a dog may be aggravated or alleviated by our attitude towards it, but we shall find it difficult to approach this hostility if we cannot recognise its source.

A dog's stance will betray whether it is undoubtedly aggressive towards an approaching person or dog: its body will stiffen, its tail become erect, the ears will stand up and the hair on its neck and back will bristle. These are obvious physical signs and will be apparent in any breed of dog regardless of its build; for example, a dog with no tail will stand erect and heighten its hip level; a dog with long or dropped ears will raise its head and the scalp will pull forwards. Such physical signs have their counterparts in human expressions: if someone causes displeasure to another human the expression of the offended person will clearly state whether he or she is hurt, upset, annoyed or downright furious. Similarly, a dog showing all the physical signs of anger is not difficult to read, for its whole body will be tight and sharp – if you could colour

At first glance these two dogs look as if they are fighting but if we look carefully we can see that the larger dog is not looking at what he is doing, his body is not prepared to either push or run, and his front legs are just resting on the other dog's head. The smaller dog's claws are resting on the big dog's side and his body is not pushing or preparing to run. This is how dog's play and is why we shouldn't try to play fight with them.

its mood it would be red! This is the dog that is prepared for a confrontation, it will not be afraid of standing its ground and its eyes will be cold and hard with a fixed stare. It would be foolhardy to confront this dog or to invade its space, for to advance upon this aggression will only anger the dog even more.

The dog that is nervous and shows aggression will show a stiffening of the body, but it will not be advancing and its ears will be pulled backwards. An aggressive dog will lower its body to pounce, but a nervously aggressive dog will lower its body and, instead of being ready to move forwards, it will almost appear to be cowering. This dog will be trying to pull back into its own space and, if the reason for its fear allows it a greater fight or flight distance, its fear will begin to subside.

Whatever reasons a dog may have for its aggression of one thing we may be certain: it is making its own decisions. It may be lacking in a strong, dependable leader, it may have had far too much of its own way, it may have suffered cruelty. Whatever the reason, its behaviour and actions will be its way not only of telling you how to handle his aggression but also why he feels the need for it.

We often condone a dog's behaviour simply by acknowledging it. The greater our reaction to a dog's aggression the more we can induce it to continue to display it. It is time now to look at Craig's progress, or rather his first few days with me.

Craig's Progress

My first impression of Craig was not of concern regarding his aggression but more of how the intentions of a handsome dog can be misleading when the body movements are not interpreted as a language. There was no mistaking how good-looking Craig was, but every fibre of his being screamed, 'Look at me, I'm important!' His owners, however, saw him as being cuddly and sweet; they knew him as a puppy when he was, no doubt, cuddly and sweet and they had retained this image of him through to his adulthood. Consequently every time Craig 'spoke' to them in a demanding tone they saw it as a request and obeyed.

Craig's problems? Stalking, fighting other dogs, attacking his owners in their own home and, of course, the obvious one of pulling on a lead and no recall. If the last two had been addressed in his formative months, any notions Craig may have had of promoting himself to pack leader would have been squashed, quietly and firmly. Craig expected attention and he intended to have it, so I totally ignored him. I took his lead, turned my back and walked away, he had no choice but to follow. He was put into a clean pen with a bowl of fresh water and left to think about his surroundings.*

Why Did Craig Show No Hostility Toward Me?

Why should he? I had shown none toward him; on the contrary, I had barely acknowledged him and so I was no threat. I had not offered a confrontation but I was not prepared to negotiate. By turning away from him I had taken away a threat or a negotiation. Do not jump to conclusions now about how I may be very brave, very foolish or able to talk to dogs where others cannot. I am none of these, I had taken on the responsibility of the dog, so being brave did not come into it, and if it did I would also have been admitting fear and he would have sensed it. Foolish? Probably, but it was me or destruction and he deserved a chance. There is no secret in understanding any animal; we understand humans (well, most of them) and human language because we live with each other, so all we are doing is learning to 'think dog' to enable us to communicate with them. Craig was extremely aggressive, rehabilitation has taken years and he is still with me as he will always have his 'trigger' memories of the past. The reason why he came to me was because he was beyond normal rehabilitation. I would never expect nor advise anyone without experience to try and deal with the level of aggression Craig came to me with. But by monitoring his progress we can see what a dog expects, why it expects it and how necessary it is to recognise the dog's language and thereby avoid the occurrence of cases such as Craig's.

This is Craig, our cover dog. Several weeks into his rehabilitation and faced with the same situation of a stranger with a camera he is showing less dominance and more of a warning. His ears are pulled back, his teeth are showing, but his lip is not drawn up in a snarl and his eyes, though focused, are not hard and cold as they are on the cover. Craig is learning to think before he acts.

CHAPTER SUMMARY

Before we can deal with aggression we need to be able to identify whether it is manifested through nerves or dominance.

Without realising it, we can induce aggression in our own dogs or in approaching dogs by incorrect body language.

Not all dogs welcome attention from strangers.

It is important that we understand and respect a dog's personal space so that we can protect it from unwelcome invasions of privacy by strangers.

CHAPTER 3

HOW AGGRESSION DEVELOPS

A dog is born with natural instincts that develop as it matures. Within the pack environment they will be developed to enable the dog to take part in the providing of food and sustaining the future of the pack. As with the human animal, some instincts are more pronounced than others: one child may be good at drawing and another at writing, together they could produce a magazine. One adult may be good at cookery skills, another at communicating, together they could run a restaurant. In the canine pack one dog may excel at searching for prey, one at hypnotising it and one at killing it. There is no room for argument as to who should do what since the future of the pack depends on good, strong providers, therefore each dog must use its strongest instinct in order to provide a well-balanced hunting party.

YOU CANNOT CHANGE A DOG

There are many things in this world we are able to change, but there are some we cannot and some we should not even want to try to. A dog is a dog, it will never be a human being, this is a fact we cannot change and should not want to change, but we do often forget that the little bundle we cuddle as a puppy is a dog. It has canine needs and canine instincts and it will be seeking canine guidance. While in its

mother's care it will have been receiving such guidance and it would expect to grow into the adolescent pack, then receiving guidance from the elders. When it goes to its new 'human' home its natural expectations have not changed, its environment has and its pack has but it still needs adult canine supervision. It is when a dog has not received any familiar pack rules from its human pack and has not been given a pack leader to depend on and to answer to that problems arise. A dog is a dog and it does not matter if it is of a very small breed or a very large one it still has canine instincts.

If a dog's most prevalent instinct is to use its teeth, then in the pack it would be an asset since it would be able to kill the prey. If the human pack allows this dog to chew and tug things they are actually nurturing the very instinct that will eventually get the dog into trouble in the eyes of human society. But remember that to the dog it is natural. This does not mean that a dog that likes to use its teeth is potentially an aggressive one, far from it, but it does mean that if its behaviour is not properly harnessed and brought back into balance then he will believe that you want him to be aggressive.

BEING REALISTIC

We have to be realistic when we are training dogs and the first thing we have to learn to accept is that we cannot both have our cake and

Playing ball with a dog can be great fun but it needs to be controlled, if a dog gets over excited its behaviour can suddenly change. This dog is playing calmly and amusing itself by rolling the ball.

eat it. We cannot play tugging games, encourage chewing, allow a dog freedom to make its own decisions and then expect it to make only the decisions we would like. If the owner does not make the rules the dog will; it will see itself as the leader of the pack, and when it jumps up at people and attacks other dogs what is it doing wrong? Its owner will know that it is wrong in human society but the dog has not been given the appropriate guidance and therefore it believes that it is making the correct decisions.

If the dog is of a dominant nature it will make decisions because it wants to; if it is of a more submissive nature it will make decisions because it feels that it has no choice. I make no apologies for the fact that I believe tugging games and the toys to go with them are not necessary; the general theory is that the human starts and stops the game, but why play this game? We now know that a puppy or a young dog will expect adult guidance, this will be to encourage the dog to use its best instincts for survival, but we do not need

When dogs get over excited they can become aggressive with the ball, and this little dog has made a good job of puncturing hers. It may seem harmful but it can have repercussions if they transfer this behaviour to other things.

this in the pet home. In fact, except in certain and rare instances, we do not need it at all. If a dog's natural instinct is to use its teeth it will take very little on the part of an unsuspecting human to teach this dog unwittingly that using its teeth and being aggressive are acceptable.

Not everything is black and white, there have to be shades of grey and the grey area in the game of 'tuggy' is that many people and

dogs take part in it, enjoy it and come to no harm. However, some dogs will have been educated not to use their teeth in an aggressive manner and there are many dog handlers who are familiar with the different temperaments of dogs and are confident in their training of them. But I still question the need to play a game in which the dog uses its teeth in preference to a mind game. It may seem like fun in the beginning, but there is little fun in

Dogs can soon progress from chewing a ball to destroying soft toys, if they can do it to their own toys they can do it to a child's teddy. Then they can progress to socks, towels and even furniture. When a dog shows signs of being destructive see it as a warning flag, take away the soft toys, keep him calm and go back to basic training and boundaries.

having your hand or your arm bitten, even if it is an accident, and it is serious when a dog bites a child and, as a result, may have to be destroyed. We are not pulling punches here, we are dealing with aggression and aggression is dangerous. If any form of training or game is even remotely capable of inducing aggression then it cannot be acceptable. Not all dog owners are confident trainers and not all owners are able to 'read' a dog's intentions in time to prevent bad habits from forming, yet many of the things that may induce aggression are available to all dog owners.

It is not unusual to see dogs tugging at their leads with their teeth and in many cases they are encouraged to do this as part of a game. This kind of 'fun' induces excitement in the dog that may often verge on hysteria. A dog in this kind of mood is not thinking and it can quickly relate the action of tugging and the growling noises that can accompany this action with the basic instinct of attacking its prey. If this seems exaggerated and that it is really only a harmless game then let us look at a possible scenario. A dog is used to tugging on a lead or a certain kind of toy; it may be under perfect control when it is with its handler or it may be a dominant dog, in either case it is still having a primeval instinct nurtured. Unexpectedly, a child holding or waving something similar in appearance to the lead or toy confronts the dog and the dog makes a grab for the article. At this stage it may be harmless, but when the child screams and the adults shout and pull that instinct can really show itself and the dog will see the child as prey and the adults as the competing pack, and the 'harmless' tug has now become an attack. Remember that we

Some dogs love to sit quietly watching television, but young dogs can get wound up by the movement on screen and jump up at it. If not corrected they can damage both themselves and the television but they are also showing signs of aggression in your home.

cannot expect a dog to think or act like a human being. It is our responsibility to see the world through the dog's eyes and to try our utmost to prevent any misunderstandings from arising within our 'pack' that could lead to the harming of any human and the eventual destruction of the dog. It may be harsh, but it is factual: if you are reading this book you

are either already dealing with an aggressive dog or you are anxious to make sure that you do not condone or exacerbate any aggressive tendencies in your dog. This means facing the fact that, as humans, we do sometimes, albeit unwittingly, involve our dogs in games that transfer the wrong message to them. This, in turn, may lead to an undesirable instinct

There's no reason why a dog shouldn't be amused by the television, but just as you wouldn't let a child sit directly in front of the screen or hit it, a dog needs to learn to view from a distance. If he's reluctant to sit back provide a mat a few feet away for him to sit on and if he still insists on creeping forwards put a lead on him and keep him by your feet.

rising to the surface, and all dogs have them, make no mistake about that.

What seems harmless in a puppy can be dangerous when that puppy grows up, and let us not forget that a puppy grows quickly. It may be small and fluffy when it is brought into the home, but in a few months it will be adolescent, and if it is not educated as a puppy it will turn into a problem teenager and then an irresponsible adult.

When we talk about the young dog as a young child we can often more easily relate to its growing stages. When I carefully explain to

the owners of a problem dog that their young pup has been allowed to be bad-mannered and that this has resulted in a wayward adolescent they find it quite easy to see the comparison. Most adults can feel for the traumas of adolescence and the way that teenagers behave without needing much encouragement – after all, it is an age that we have all experienced. There is a similarity between the human adolescent and the adolescent dog: both will test their elders while they strive to define new boundaries; but there the similarities end. It is possible to converse with a

Once wound up and over excited the sweetest and calmest dog can lose its temper and act unpredictably. A little bit of hand wrestling and this dog has had enough!

human being; he knows the rules of his society and the consequences of disobeying them. Even if he has lacked parental guidance he should still have some sense of what is implied by education and employment and what is expected of them even if they choose to rebel. A dog understands what it is taught and in the pack the elders will have guided and reprimanded it until a responsible adult emerges. But if a dog enters a human pack, does not understand its language and is not given an easy-to-follow rule book, then how can it reach maturity as a sensible dog?

MAKING EXCUSES

Explaining to the owner of a problem dog that it is an adolescent is easy; pointing out that the dog is bad-mannered is a little harder. But most owners can understand the rules of good manners and this is all that most of

Dogs can be territorial, and while its good to know your dog won't just let anyone into your home, allowing him to keep standing guard at a door can lead to him to not letting anyone in at all.

them are seeking for their dogs. Not all owners aspire to win trophies in competitions; they just want a well-mannered companion. While they are telling me about the bad habits their dogs display they may have children sitting as good as gold, listening to all we are saying and displaying impeccable manners. I will point out to the owners that they have raised well-mannered children but then ask what would they have said to their children if they had wandered around the room, interrupting the conversation and touching ornaments? Nearly all parents will say that their children would never have done that, they knew not to. So why is the dog doing it? The answer is invariably the same: the dog does not understand. Of course it does not – it has not been taught! We are often far more lenient with a dog than with a child, yet communication with a child is such that we can apologise for

misunderstandings, we can make clear in our language what we want and we can change what we say from one day to the next and explain the reasons for this. A dog will understand what it first learns from us, and, if we repeat words, allow it to do things in its own time and fail to explain our rules correctly then it will respond to our indecision, and, of course, its response will be 'I'm in charge!' It is a natural reaction to defend one's dog, but in so doing we are usually making excuses, sometimes for our dogs and sometimes for ourselves. It is no good excusing a dog because it does not understand or it is too young; it will understand what it has been taught, and if this education has led it to believe that it has a senior pack position then the dog cannot be blamed. It may sound harsh, but we must accept that excuses do not make the dog; they serve only as time-wasters when we should be getting on

There are a lot dogs that play with tuggy toys but it is allowing a dog to think it is fine to be aggressive with something attached to a human being. It doesn't matter who stops and who starts the game the dog has to show some kind of aggression in order to play the game. Following photographs show how this can go sadly wrong.

with the job of educating the dog. Remember that we are learning about aggression here and aggression does not rear its head without a reason and that reason will always stem from a human influence. Be it breeding, rearing, handling, training, toys, food – any or all of these will contribute to the dog's character and temperament.

HOW PROBLEMS ARISE

There are many contributory factors when aggression is manifested in a dog and quite often they are born of innocence. It may seem quite harmless to provide a dog with a plentiful supply of 'toys', especially when there is such a choice on offer, and if they are readily available it would appear that they must not only be harmless but necessary.

A saying I am well-known for is 'think dog' and I endeavour to try and help owners to understand what their dogs are thinking. I see little point in telling people how to train or how to rehabilitate a dog without explaining what they are doing. It is undoubtedly easier telling them what to do rather than to explain why it should be done, but it does not help them to understand their dogs. So let us look at the toys on offer and how they can develop unwelcome instincts in a dog, but how they can also be used to enhance the desirable ones.

This is a large dog playing a game of tug, she is not aggressive and she is not putting a lot of effort into the tug but look at the power in her body if she should decide to do so.

Many toys make noises; they usually squeak and have a great deal of appeal as a toy box 'must'. If I point out to you that a rabbit or a mouse will squeak if a dog catches it you will be able to see how a dog may actually view that 'harmless', squeaky toy. The act of making the toy squeak in a controlled, almost humorous way is not harmful; in fact, both dog and owner can have fun with it. But if the squeaking is made by the dog running, jumping, chewing and destroying the toy and in so doing becoming almost hysterical, then nothing but harm can come from such a form of play. The dog is not only being allowed to destroy, it is being encouraged to use its teeth and its natural survival instinct to use its teeth on its prey is being aroused. This seemingly harmless and often amusing antic of 'killing' the toy can cause the arousal of aggression in the dog. It starts as a game, just as it would in the pack, and it carries

it through into adolescence and, if the owner is not the unmistakable pack leader, the dog will take over and use its new-found aggression to obtain dominance.

So a squeaky toy may actually encourage the scales to tilt unfavourably towards aggression by encouraging the instinct we least want our dogs to show to rise to the surface. But what other instincts do dogs have and how do they learn good manners in the pack? Puppies will learn to seek, to track, to outwit and to wait their turn: these are all things that can be taught by an owner in a way that the pup will understand and, in so doing, will not only be having fun but will also be learning. The pup or the older dog must wait before taking the toy; it can learn to find it – quietly, with no hysteria; it can learn to sniff it out, and it can learn to make it squeak on command. One of the best games with a puppy is to sit on the

Here we can see what happens if the dog misses its target! She is not aggressive but neither is she a machine, she is a dog and sometimes they get it wrong. What if this had been a child, or someone in the park with a skipping rope and an over-excited dog made a grab for it? I have done far too many consultations where this has happened for me to not shudder when I think of the consequences to child and dog. Big dog or small, a bite – even accidental – can do serious damage.

floor playing mind games. If you communicate with the pup and allow it to develop its own game rather than tell it how to play, and then join in by literally playing it at its own game, you will have lots of fun and will be very subtly educating it at the same time.

A ball is a favourite, most dogs have one, but what should a dog do with it? I suppose it sounds like a silly question, balls are meant to be thrown and retrieved, but who says so? We throw balls, we also kick them and we catch

them, but a dog does not know this, we teach it, and quite often we then complain because the dog is constantly 'bringing' the ball or it will not go on a walk without its ball. But it did not learn this by itself; it will have actually been taught that a ball plays an important role in its life. Yet if you show a puppy a ball for the very first time it will be suspicious of it! So roll the ball and allow him to investigate it and see whether he can invent a game of his own. Do not encourage a dog to chew a ball or to be possessive with it; the 'no-teeth' command can be introduced at a very early age and will prevent the dog from bursting a football when it is a little older. In fact, a football should be rolled, pushed and manoeuvred, not bitten. A ball of any size can be a wonderful tool for educating a dog, but it can also be a push button to stimulate hysteria if it is not used with care.

DIET

Diet can be a strong contributory factor to aggression in a dog; the actual type of food itself will not instigate it but the energy content of the diet needs to be taken into consideration. If a dog's energy intake is in excess of its requirements it will become overactive, which may lead to hyperactivity; this, in turn, can exacerbate any bad habits and can make the dog difficult to train. A diet appropriate for the dog's growth rate and energy level is vital; if a dog is not working or engaged in strenuous exercise it does not need food that will fuel its energy. If a dog is showing signs of dominance or aggression then it needs its food intake to be cut to a very low energy level in order to enable the owner to address the problem rather than have to tussle with a dog 'drunk' on high protein.

While considering the diet of an aggressive or unruly dog it is also worth remembering that not all react in the same manner to particular foods. One dog may be on a high-energy diet, rich in protein and red meat and happily devouring biscuits in a variety of colours, but this diet could be like a time bomb to another animal. Whenever I question the diet of a problem dog I am usually confronted with a challenge from the owner along the lines of 'My friend's dog is on the same diet as mine and he doesn't have a problem.' Quite so, *he* does not have a problem and so there is no need to question the diet (or the behaviour) of *his* dog. But when a dog has a problem all avenues must be explored and the first one is food: a high percentage of problem dogs improve when their diet is changed. This does not mean that all diets need to be reduced in energy content, nor that to change the diet will retrain the dog, but if a dog has a problem the correct diet can make it easier to handle – rather like a car, it will perform better on the correct fuel. To train an unruly or dominant dog or one with aggressive tendencies is extremely difficult if the dog is almost intoxicated with high-energy food.

LEAD WALKING

It may sound silly that lead walking can induce aggression but it is a fact. Walking correctly on a lead will not cause aggression, but how many dogs do actually walk correctly? Of course, it all depends on what is considered correct and, in general, the dog walking at the side of its owner, often with its head just a little in front, is considered correct. But is it? To humans it may seem acceptable and it is pleasant to have your dog walking companionably at the side of you. But the problem is that it does not always happen; quite often, if it does happen, it takes time and a lot of pulling and tugging until eventually both dog and owner compromise. However, if lead walking is taught in a way that the dog understands it is relatively easy, does not involve any pulling and a walk becomes a pleasure, not one long argument.

Let us look at it from the dog's point of view for a moment. Its natural instinct is that of a pack animal and, when a pack is on the move, who do we normally expect to see in the front? The pack leader. We can also make similar comparisons to a pride of lions: the pack leader is the undisputed 'boss', the one who leads the way, makes the decisions and protects. If the leader were to be further back he would lose both credibility and respect; in all probability he could no longer be leader, someone else would soon be making the decisions and thus command the respect of the rest of the pack. There you have it in a nutshell, and, when we look at the pack in a simple and readily understandable way, we can see what the dog would expect of a leader. We can also see how the dog would assume the role itself if its handler did not appear to be a strong or capable leader.

Ensuring that the dog knows its pack place means that it must understand that, when told to do so, it must walk behind its handler, not in front nor at the side. In this position the dog is a part of the pack and not the leader and you do not need an army of dogs for them to qualify as a pack: whether you have several dogs or few, they are your pack, one dog constitutes a pack. If you find this hard to accept, remember that if your dog decides to assume the role of leader it will automatically demote you to being a pack member and it will not need to replicate you to do so. It will be quite content to make you do all the things a good pack member should do. In fact, you will be making life extremely easy for it when you allow it walk in front and pull on the lead, since, in its eyes, it is not just pulling you, it is keeping you behind. Once a dog understands that its place is behind you in pack position you can invite it to walk at your side or in front of you, and it will all be done with your consent.

So why does this make a difference to a dog's behaviour? To begin with, if the dog knows its place in the pack it will leave it to its handler to make the decisions. This means that, should it be faced with a 'threat' such as another dog, it will allow its handler to sort out the situation and to advise it how to behave. It also means that, should a 'threat' appear on the scene unexpectedly, the dog can be called into pack position immediately and the handler will then be between the dog and the threat, in a protective position. Few dogs that are dominant or show aggressive tendencies are good on a lead and nearly all of them have a poor recall. Once again, we need to look at life through the eyes of the dog and realise that when it is pulling on a lead it is taking its owner on a walk, not being taken. When the handler pulls the dog back, the desired reaction of making the dog understand that it must not pull is reversed. For while the handler is pulling back the dog is pulling forwards, and thus any words it hears, such as 'Heel', are associated, not with being pulled back to heel, but with pulling the handler forwards. Subliminally the dog is learning that 'heel' means pull, this, in turn, condones the dog making decisions and telling the handler what to do, and promotes it to pack leader. Now we can see why it is important for a dog to know who is the leader and where his pack position is, and why a dog pulling on a lead can actually see the decision to be aggressive as his right.

Craig's Progress

After the initial 'insult' of being ignored, Craig began to be inquisitive and was allowed to wander out of his pen and take in his surrounding, while still being confined to the inside of a building. To ignore a dog is not something to be undertaken lightly or without good reason. The concept is for the dog to understand its place and its worthiness, or rather unworthiness, and this technique is sometimes advocated for dogs that jump and fuss when their owners enter the house. This is not the time to ignore your dog, for it will be greeting you in a manner you have already allowed or even encouraged, and, although suddenly to ignore it in this situation may have the desired effect in the short term, in the longer term it may have serious repercussions. It will eventually dawn on the dog that its owner is no longer pleased to see it and does not welcome its advances any more. Yes, that is exactly how the dog will see it, and it will stay in its bed or out of the way, but it will feel rebuffed; it will feel rejected and it may harbour anxiety or anger. So the long-term effect, and I have had many such cases in recent years, can show itself by the dog either cowering from its owner when he or she enters the house or, in the case of a dominant dog, actually showing aggression towards its owner. 'You choose to ignore me, so I won't let you in!' The dog in your home is already in your pack; if it is the leader then you need to demote it; if you are the leader then you do not have a problem – the dog that greets you is your dog, so why not say 'Hello' when you enter your home? If you are in control of your dog you simply ask him to sit and wait until you are prepared to fuss over him; if you are not in control there is little point in ignoring him as he is perfectly entitled to ignore you.

Craig was a newcomer to my pack, and for me to negotiate or confront him would have meant that I was willing to fight and was prepared to throw him out. By ignoring him when we first met I gained his respect and he realised that the position of leader was not up for grabs. You can only get away with ignoring a dog when he first enters your pack, and he would expect this. But at any other time it is open to the dog to misinterpret your reasons and, when he draws his own conclusions, they may not be what you wanted.

CHAPTER SUMMARY

It is important to be able to identify some of the things that may exacerbate or even cause aggression.

Diet can play an important part in a dog's welfare. A high-energy diet not fully utilised in growing or working may make a young or problem dog difficult to train. If a dog is allowed to chew toys it may become destructive, and pulling on a lead may encourage it to take control. In such situations barking or growling may induce hysteria.

When working to gain your dog's respect, think carefully before you use the technique of ignoring him; this may have an adverse effect on some dogs in certain situations.

CHAPTER 4

DEALING WITH AGGRESSION

I thought hard about the title for this chapter, since we have seen how and why a dog may become aggressive and have now reached the point where we have to turn the dog around, from being a problem to being manageable. No form of aggression is acceptable and none must be ignored; it is not straightforward training and therefore it must be dealt with. If we deal with the aggression we can train the dog, but first we must see the dog and its aggression as separate elements and then deal with them as a whole. They must be separated so that the real dog can be seen through its veil of aggression; thus the dog within can be encouraged to emerge. If all you see is an aggressive dog you cannot know what you are looking for behind this behaviour.

Let us assume that we have a dog showing aggression towards its owner; it may happen when it is being fed, when it is taken out for a walk or simply when it feels that its human (there is a clue) has displeased it. Or it may be when it is confronted with something that it is worried about: another dog, a visitor or a car journey. Or it may be acting protectively towards its owner, children, toys or even another dog. In each of these possible situations the dog is in charge; whether it wants to be or not is a different matter and is something the owner must discover before any measures can be taken to re-educate the dog. We have to ask the dog its reasons for being aggressive

before we can explain to it that it is neither a needed nor an acceptable attitude. Of course, we are not going to sit around a table and put a questionnaire to the dog, but neither should we rush in and assume that we know what the dog is feeling. Patience and understanding are needed. I know that these are difficult requirements when a dog is showing aggression, but rushing in and trying to 'sort it out' will only make matters worse.

The dog showing aggression with regard to its food and going for a walk is definitely seeing itself as the pack leader; it will be displaying dominant aggression, which is not hard to recognise. It will be clearly showing signs of being in charge, doing what it wants when it wants to. It will expect its owner to feed it and then to move out of its space until it needs something else. But – and it is a large one, where the owner must be honest – how did the dog come to be promoted to leader? No dog suddenly decides how it is going to behave; the signs will have been there for the owner to see but will not have been noticed. The dog will have begun to demand its food at a certain time, instead of being appreciative of what is provided for it. It will also have eaten its food when and how it wanted to, gulping it, leaving some until later or maybe just sitting and guarding it. This should have been observed and attended to, but quite often when they are pointed out they were obvious at the time – but only when you know what

Which of these two dogs do think is the most dominant? The one on the left is relaxed, his body and face are greeting sideways and his expression is not hostile, but he has entered her space. The one on the right has turned her head so she is greeting face to face, her eye is strong and her body is leaning to the side ready to make the next move.

The next move! She turns on the dog before he has chance to get away and without biting, she aims for his neck as a warning. Sequence photographs can provide a lot of information and are over in seconds, as was this incident. She made is quite clear she wants her space and he was happy to trot away unharmed.

to expect. For example, it may seem nice to have a routine whereby the dog is fed at the same time each day, and with some it is an advantage since it provides a degree of regularity. However, many dogs, and particularly the dominant ones, will begin to 'clock watch' and, before their unsuspecting owners have realised it, the dogs are in control, with their owners rushing to get food ready or even trying to beat the dogs by serving it sooner. Such a dog will soon begin to lay the law down as to how and when it wants to be fed, and then begin to organise the rest of its life. It will pull on its lead, or – and this is a common reaction of owners who tend to say something along the lines of 'My dog doesn't have a problem with pulling since it is rarely on the lead' – it will do as it pleases.

It may all seem trivial, so much so that it has not been noticed, and if your dog is not aggressive it may appear that pointers such as these cannot contribute towards aggression, but they most certainly can. There is nothing wrong with a dog being off the lead provided that it appreciates that its owner is allowing this freedom as a concession. The dog must understand that the owner both can and will restrict the freedom to the 'pack' space only (the space behind the leader) if not shown respect. The owner of the dog is then making it quite clear who is in control; the regimes of feeding and going for a walk have changed little and only very subtly, but enough for the dog to understand its position. The leader provides food and there is no argument as to the quality of it, or the time at which, or the manner in which it is served. A walk is when and where the leader designates, and if the area is safe the dog can have freedom, but if there is risk of an unknown threat the dog must travel in the security of the pack space. Freedom, by the way, does not mean that the dog may career off miles into the distance, chasing rabbits and birds, and come back only when it thinks fit; it means that the dog remains within a sensible distance of its handler, certainly within earshot and keeps in communication with him.

The dog that shows apprehension with regard to other dogs and people and is nervous when confronted with an unusual situation (and remember that what is normal to us may be both unusual and disturbing to a dog) will be displaying nervous aggression. Far from dictating about its eating regime, this dog will probably not be happy about eating in public nor about most situations its owner introduces it to. This kind of dog probably appears to be obedient, but if much soul-searching is done by the owner he may realise that the dog is not so much obedient as too nervous to push ahead and be disobedient. Unlike the dominant dog who needs to know who the pack leader is in order to keep him in check, the nervous dog needs to know who the pack leader is in order to feel secure and protected.

The possessive dog will display aggression to protect whatever it considers itself to be in control of; to begin with, it may be its food, but even this small display of possessiveness can lead to greater things. Possessiveness can also be directed toward the owner, the owner's children or even the pet cat or gerbil. Unfortunately, both the owner and the family often unwittingly encourage this kind of aggression. It may seem pleasant and even flattering when a dog is protective, but protection can be confused with possessiveness and this is not only insulting (it questions the owner's capability to be protective) but can and does lead to aggression, which is dangerous.

THE FOUNDATION OF AGGRESSION

There are several explanations for aggressiveness, but fundamentally all are born of either nervous aggression or dominant aggression. A dog being possessive is either nervous and feels the need to protect or is dominant, where protection is only a short distance from controlling. It is impossible to build without a foundation. I remember once watching a well-known artist painting a picture of Sitting Bull; he created a young, strong brave, but when I went back a week later Sitting Bull was an old man. When I asked him what he had done to the painting and why had he made the great chief old, he smiled and said, 'I never intended him to be young, the old man has the experience of life in his face, but how could I paint an old man without first creating the foundation of his youth?' Wise words: if you build a house with a poor foundation it will eventually weaken and repairs will be difficult to carry out without going back to the foundations to rebuild it; but a house with a strong foundation will weather many storms and suffer little. If a dog has a problem there is no doubt that the foundation of its training will have been weak, and just as a weak building must be strengthened from the base upwards so must the dog's re-education go back to basics.

As far as I am concerned, there are four non-negotiable commands for dogs and, if you doubt the importance of these, think carefully of how they work. A dog must stop, stay, come back and walk behind when it is told to, and it must do it on the first time of asking. These commands are not a part of any training regime, they are not connected in any way to competition training and they will not detract from any formal training; they are plain, common-sense good manners and dogs understand them. If a dog will not stop nor stay when it is told to you will find it difficult to communicate with it since it will be concentrating on anything but what you want it to do. If a dog will not come back when it is called it is an accident waiting to happen. I do not just mean that it may chase a rabbit or jump up at a stranger, showering him with mud, I mean that it may run in front of a car, killing itself and causing an accident. If a dog does not understand that it should show you the courtesy and respect of staying in the pack space behind you until it is invited to move forwards then the other three commands are not even worth attempting.

Respect

Respect from your dog is essential for without it you cannot be the pack leader. I have heard all the arguments in favour of allowing a dog to enjoy its youth, to be able to play when it wants, have toys at random, have the run of the house and so on. I have also heard the reasons for misbehaviour excused by comments such as 'He's only a year old', 'He enjoys tugging at the lead', and an especially good one, 'We didn't get a dog not to be able to enjoy it.' But these comments are not made by people who have well-mannered dogs, they are made by owners whose dogs are quite happily chewing holes in their shoes while they are telling me how the dogs just need a little time. There is no such thing as a well-mannered problem dog and a problem dog does nothing to enhance the relationship between itself and its owner.

Every dog should enjoy its youth, it should be able to use its imagination to play some kind of game and, provided that it accepts the house rules, you can allow it to have access to any part of the house that you want. A dog should be well-mannered from puppyhood, tugging on a lead is not giving cause for enjoyment so much as stimulating a rush of adrenaline. A well-mannered, well-behaved dog is a joy in itself. So now that we have looked at and rejected all the arguments and excuses let us get down to finding out how we are going to deal with an aggressive dog and make it more respectful.

GOLDEN RULES

In the remainder of this chapter we are going to look at some of the rules and how to apply them. In the next chapter we shall put them into practice with both dominant and nervous dogs.

Let us look at life through the puppy's eyes first. If a puppy is allowed to chew its toys it will see no reason why it cannot chew your 'toys': socks on the radiator, shoes, anything you may leave round for its inspection. If a

A lovely greeting and a happy dog but what seems the smallest thing can change a dog's perception.

A different position of the hands and two fingers with plaster covering fresh wounds. The smell of blood, the disinfectant and sudden change of position and the dog's approach changes. In order to understand our dogs we need to be aware of how they use their senses, their keen hearing and sense of smell help them to protect themselves. In this type of instance would a dog have been aggressive or thinking it was protecting itself if it had attacked the hand?

puppy uses its teeth for anything other than eating, then at what point are you going to say that it has to stop doing this? A puppy tugging at a toy and playing a game with you may seem like good fun, but in the puppy pack it is learning about survival, competition and how to use its teeth for killing. It is the responsibility of the owner to teach it how to understand its canine culture without encouraging its survival instincts to rise to the surface. Puppies will tug on a lead with their teeth, they will play with and then try to tug at your feet as you walk, and they will try and catch your hand with their teeth. When they are little it may seem harmless, but puppies grow quickly and, if you allow them to think that they can do this just once, they will do it again later and may hurt someone. So golden rule number one is never to encourage a puppy to use its teeth.

Rule number two is that a dog should be taught to walk behind you first and at the side of you second. If a dog is in front of you without your permission you will either be pulled forwards or you will have to pull it back. You have now shown weakness, for a leader does not allow its pack to go in front without permission and, as you lose credibility as a leader, your dog gains it. Remember the four non-negotiable commands? Now you can use them: make your dog sit and wait until you are a lead length in front of him and then quietly give him permission to move. Do not use a recall command and do not use the heel command; in fact, do not use anything you are likely to need at a later date. As soon as he makes a move forward tell him to sit again. Keep repeating this action until the dog is expecting you to keep making him sit; at this point he will stand and move slowly forwards and now is the time to tell him what he is doing. This is subliminal training: you get the dog to do what you want it to do and then provide it with a word for the action; it is far easier than trying to make a dog do something when it has not got a clue what the human word for the action means. I always recommend a word such as 'back' or 'behind' for the pack space and then the more universal 'heel' command may be used to bring the dog to your side.

Golden rules numbers three and four. If your dog does not have the foundation of a sit-and-stay then training must begin immediately to make him understand that these commands are not negotiable. Do not attempt to teach them where there are distractions or where he is likely to try and assert his dominance toward other dogs or people. Teach these important lessons of manners in your own home and make sure that you do not negotiate. It's surprising how many people do not realise that they are negotiating nor how subtly their dog takes control: a little twitch of the shoulder tells you that your dog is about to move and, instead of insisting that he stays, it is easier to give him permission to move. But which came first: the command from you or did he actually tell you to give him the command to move?

Before we can deal with the aggression we must find out the reason for it and, in so doing, we must also be brutally honest about any past negotiations with our dog regarding rules, negotiations that will have encouraged him to make decisions that belong to hierarchy. If your dog is a rescue dog you will not be worrying about the negotiations *you* have made; this will make it easier for you to introduce your dog to your pack with a brand new set of rules. However, you will have to be careful that your newcomer does not cajole you into being an easy target for demotion and you will also have to wait until the negotiations of previous owners show themselves. This calls for extreme vigilance on your part since the dog will expect that he has the right to take over your pack if he is dominant and a nervous dog will be less trusting and more introvert each time it enters a new pack. Your pack rules must come across loud and clear in the first few hours of allowing a rescue into your domain. Remember that you personally will be taking a rescue dog into your home to provide it with love, security and safety, but this must be made clear to him in his language not yours. Communicating with a rescue for the first time will be explored at a later stage when we understand more about the way to impress our leadership qualities on a dog.

Rule number five. A dog without an instant recall is a dog making decisions, pleasing itself and showing absolutely no respect for any leadership other than its own. Ultimately, as I have already said, it may cause an accident; but we must never underestimate the seriousness of any refusal by a dog to come back when called, for what may not appear to be a fraught situation could soon turn into one. The dog running through woods may meet something you are not even aware of, it could be a rabbit in which case it will begin what is usually a futile chase. If the dog were to meet a larger animal, such as a deer or sheep, and give chase the results could be disastrous. A horse could throw its rider if the dog startled it and gave chase, and walkers who were allergic to dogs would not be happy if an out-of-control, bad-mannered dog jumped all over them. So whatever an owner may not deem important could soon change into a major issue if he cannot guarantee that he could recall his dog in any circumstances.

The main reason for an inconsistent recall is failure to explain to the dog what is required and also to teach the word in a way that the dog can understand. Let us assume the recall is 'Come here'; it is no good calling 'Come here' to a dog that is clearly not going to come, all you are doing is teaching the dog that it does not have to do as you say first time. If you want your dog to come to you first time you must make sure that he understands this by ensuring that he does not get a second call. If he does not come first time then go to him and fetch him back to the spot you were on when you called him. If he is going to run away when you do this or treat it as a game, where are you going wrong? He should want to run to you, not away from you and to teach good manners is not a game, it is not optional, it is mandatory. Training should be fun and I accept that many owners use titbits and toys as rewards for a dog doing as it has been told. In my opinion if bribes have to be used to ensure

good manners then there is something wrong. Using such incentives for 'extra-curricular' activities, such as training for competition or teaching tricks, may be acceptable, but I want and, indeed, expect, my dog to do things for me out of love and respect. I do not expect to have to plead with it to respect me; I command respect by the very fact I provide for it and as such can have fun in sharing our lives, not our toys. I do not deny that toys may be beneficial, for my dogs know all about balls, although they do devise their own games. However, toys are not to be made so important in a dog's life that it lives for them, cannot go on a walk without one and will only do certain things if a toy is on offer. You should be the most important thing in your dog's life and toys are not a substitute or a bribe; they are a stopgap while you are otherwise occupied. It is human beings who need to get toys into perspective, not dogs, for dogs can and do live without toys; they are not an essential part of their well-being and dogs are not untrainable without them.

The fun part of training for a dog is its pleasing you; if it does not get enjoyment in this way then once again we have a pointer indicating weakness in the leadership role. A dog will get great satisfaction from hearing the words 'Good dog' spoken quietly and with pride, for a dog will serve and give pleasure unconditionally. When praise is given in an excited manner it will incite a copycat reaction from the dog, which will soon be jumping about ecstatically and have quite forgotten what the praise was for in the first place. Keep it quiet and calm and the dog will still be waiting and concentrating on the next request. The time to let go and share a whoop of joy is when the training session is over.

If your dog is failing in an instant recall you must go back to basics. Begin by putting a light line on him around the house and keep calling him to you; call once only and use the line to make sure that he comes immediately. Tell him that you are pleased and then let him go again. Graduate to the garden and eventually to further afield. Alternate calling him to you with reminding him that he must go no further: a pack dog accepts his pack boundaries, and if you are going to allow him to keep wandering further away he will be determining his own limits. A dog setting his own boundaries is taking over the leadership. A circle of about 25yd in diameter is your pack space, and, until your dog understands the recall, he should not go beyond it. If you make up your mind to abide by this you will be consistent and in a short time you will have your dog going as far as 20yd and then waiting as he expects a reminder to go no further. If you are half-hearted about this you will be inconsistent and your dog will never see you as the strong person you need to be. The importance of good manners is often overlooked, particularly if a dog does not pose too great a problem in its formative years. However, their absence may cause major behavioural problems which, in turn, can lead to aggression.

So, if at any time any of these rules seem insignificant, think of the aggression you are trying to deal with and resolve to impress pack law firmly upon your dog.

I have not listed these rules in any order of importance, but if only one of them could be applied it would have to be the recall, for without it a dog cannot justifiably be given any freedom. But each rule is equally important and each is dependent on the others. Allowing a puppy the freedom to use its teeth as it pleases is transmitting an early message that you do not make rules. A 'pack walk' cannot be explained if the dog will not stop and listen, neither can it be enforced if the dog will not wait and allow you to walk forwards into your own space. A dog that believes that it has the right to walk in front of you and does not wait for permission to do so will already have failed to come up to scratch in one or all of the previous rules. Once again, it is easy to think that

Puppies are lovely, they are playful and cuddly but they soon grow into adults, and a child playing with a puppy can soon become at risk if they play with an adult dog the same way. These two pups are having lots of fun playing, a little bit of wrestling and mouthing, but they should be discouraged from this kind of play with humans, especially with children.

There is a sudden change in the mood when one puppy loses its temper.

Now it's getting more serious with these two, it will end up in a puppy fight which will soon be over and they will be best of friends again. This is what puppies do, it's how they play and it often ends up in a fight as they are learning new skills. If a puppy sees a child as a playmate it will not understand why it can't bite the child. This may be thought to be 'puppy nipping' but it's a pup thinking it can 'practice' its skills on its playmate. Imagine the consequences a few months later when the pup is an adult dog playfighting with a toddler!

your dog is obeying the rules, but if it is aggressive it is disobedient and if it is disobedient it is not accepting you as the pack leader. If you are not the leader it is not respecting you or it has not been taught the golden rules. A dog may sit and stay when it is told at a training class or in your garden or when you stand in a certain manner and hold your hand in a particular gesture, but this dog is answering only to certain criteria. It believes that it needs to answer to the spoken word only when it is accompanied by one of these gestures and is in a certain area. If the dog is looking around with its ears pricked up and is taking little notice of you as a person then you have been demoted to the status of a noticeboard that can be ignored if a better offer arises. That is not a pleasant feeling but it is a true interpretation, and do not be persuaded into believing that your dog must have its gaze fixed squarely on you either, for, once again, this is a human concept. A dog in the pack is not in front of the leader gazing round at him nor is it walking at his side gazing up at him, but it will be aware of his every move and will always be showing respect for him. How on earth do guide dogs, sheepdogs, search and rescue dogs and police dogs work if they have to be continually staring at their owners? I shall not labour this point because I am sure that it will now be clear what I am saying: quite simply when a dog knows you are the pack leader your requests, commands and very existence will never be ignored.

Far too many dogs that fit the behaviour criteria for competition have become so accustomed to what is necessary to compete that they have not developed the canine law of who makes the rules when not competing, therefore they make their own. This is not a slur on competitions nor any particular dog sport since they are good for both the dog and the handler, but the primary rules for a dog are pack rules. To learn these a dog must be reminded it is a dog in language it understands and humans must 'think dog' in order to convey these rules in an acceptable language to the dog.

WHERE SHOULD YOUR DOG BE LOOKING?

The answer is: where it is going! It is obvious really, but to be confident in allowing your dog to look ahead you have to be able to understand his language. If his ears are pricked up he is concentrating on what he is looking at, hence the reason for having a dog look up at you. But when a dog is looking up at its owner it is not concentrating on him, after all, he has seen him before; he is responding to and concentrating on an action he has been taught that is not a canine instinct. Do you really intend to go on a walk with your dog gazing at you all the time?

Of course not. But the dog that is educated to walk to heel only when it is looking up at its owner is not being educated to walk with respect for its owner while getting on with its own life. There is a huge difference between training for competition and teaching a dog basic good manners and it is essential that this is borne in mind when first educating your dog. Watch the ears, watch the body and watch the tail: this is your dog talking to you or ignoring you, so learn to listen to him. When he is concentrating on the way ahead with fixed gaze, pricked ears and stiffened tail you have already lost his attention, which has wandered from you to a desirable or aggressive thought. As soon as the ears go up call him back. The argument of 'if the dog had been looking at the owner in the first place the attention would not have strayed' is not applicable: after all, this is a dog and it needs to have some free time. The dog that is not allowed free time because it cannot be trusted off the lead is a dog (and an owner) with a problem. When an owner can differentiate between respectful pack rules and rules that are of human origin and can convey these to the dog in a manner the dog understands no problem will be insurmountable. Problems occur because somewhere along the way one of our species has failed in communicating with

Whether a big dog or a small one it can be very daunting when one you don't know is approaching you at full speed. This dog is not big but to a small child it could seem huge.

Because this is a big dog, and it would be a giant to a toddler, it may seem more intimidating than a smaller dog. But a dog's actions are often based on a person's reaction. Dogs can react to fear and if a child screams at an approaching dog, that dog can react adversely. A dog's size does not determine how it will react, big dogs are often softies and little dogs are as capable of biting as any dog of any size or breed.

the dog in its own language, which, in turn, makes it difficult for the dog to learn our language.

COMMUNICATING WITH YOUR DOG

It may seem obvious that communication is important when it is pointed out, but communication on our (human) terms is pointless when the dog cannot speak our language. One of the essential ingredients for a good partnership of whatever nature is communication, and if the partners do not speak the same language then greater effort must be

made to make sure that misunderstandings do not occur. I would find it hard to believe anyone who said that they had never made a mistake that gave rise to a misunderstanding between them and a dog. I know I have; in fact, I make mistakes regularly. We may all admit that we have been guilty at some time of not listening to a family member or friend, or of not placing the importance on their conversation that it may have warranted. We are not superhuman and in the case of another human being we can apologise and start again from where we left off; but, with a dog, if we have not created a bond and the means of communication it is often necessary to begin again from scratch.

Accepting that we need to be able to communicate is half of the battle, for we then, logically, have to observe and study a dog to be able to find out how best to communicate with him. This realisation now tells us that it would be wrong to try and approach a dog either physically or mentally until we have some message from him as to how he regards us and what his intentions are. It is all down to common sense; in fact, all dog training and rehabilitation should be based on common sense. A dog will not be concerned with various courses of action; it will be protecting its space until it has decided how to deal with a situation. If you force mental or physical contact with a dog it will then act on a protective instinct, and according to its genes it has every right to do so. If this then causes a dispute between human and dog a situation has arisen where you cannot rewind and start again because the dog will be suspicious of you. If in doubt, keep out, never enter a dog's space when you do not know or understand it, always make sure that you are 'reading' his language correctly, and if you are not sure do not confront him.

You need to learn your dog's language, but if you think that this may be difficult, that your dog will not listen to you, or that you do not have the time to learn the language in order

Older dogs can suddenly seem to become short tempered or even aggressive but quite often they are stiff and their bodies have aches and pains. It's important to make sure children don't try to keep playing with them. Old dogs often end up in rescues because they have suddenly started nipping a child in the family. Old or young they deserve their personal space and respect.

for you to act immediately, do not worry. Just make sure that all your communication with your dog is in a language it understands, for you must prove yourself as the pack leader by your actions.

SHOULD YOU CHASTISE?

Can there be a set rule, or rather will other people's opinions allow each owner to create his own rules? If you decide that you do not think that you should chastise your dog then someone will try to convince you that you should; and if you decide that you should there will be someone else telling you that it is wrong. It is time go back to good, old common sense. Let us assume that someone has a dominant dog that has either been aggressive or has shown aggressive tendencies. From what we have learnt so far we may deduce that the dog is, or certainly believes itself to be, the pack leader – the boss. No boss likes being demoted by an employee and no pack leader will willingly give way to a new leader, so assuredly the dog would argue. Now if that dog makes an aggressive stand and the owner reciprocates with a show of aggression, who is going to win? The owner has a 50 per cent chance of winning, but that also means a 50 per cent chance of losing the stand off; but the winner will inevitably be the loser. Let me explain: if the dog wins the argument it has reinforced its position of self-appointed leader and in doing so it has either bitten or has unnerved its owner sufficiently for him to lose all confidence. The dog may either be put down or sent to a rescue kennels. If the owner shows aggression

People often want to be far more familiar with a dog than the dog actually wants, and if the dog doesn't reciprocate they try harder. We should never force ourselves on a dog, it can respond either with aggression or fear, this dog is being submissive but is not showing fear, if the person continues it is likely to defend itself.

and wins the argument the dog may become submissive or even nervous of the owner or it will bide its time and try again.

Going back to pack rules, if the leader is challenged by a pack member he will have to stand his ground; but he has already shown weakness by allowing the situation to happen. If a leader fights he will fight to the death or will cast out the offender; a human is going to do neither and therefore a show of aggression by a human cannot be carried through as a pack leader. This, of course, depends on the severity of the challenge; within a pack it should not occur for it would be a tight unit, the leader will command respect and internal fighting should not be evident. So how do human rules hold up to the way a dog expects a pack to be organised? We argue, we negotiate and we allow insubordination; in fact, every time a dog *thinks* about obeying the golden rules rather than *abiding* by them it is subtly forcing its owner to negotiate. Unless the owner is the pack leader, in which case the dog should know better than to try to negotiate.

So what happens if the leader is called upon to show a little stern displeasure at a young insubordinate? He shows his strength by putting the dog in its place, and this is where the human term of 'scruffing' comes from. But in my opinion it is grossly misinterpreted and can lead to someone's getting bitten and the ruination of a dog.

WHAT IS 'SCRUFFING'?

Scruffing is a term sometimes used to describe the practice of taking hold of the loose coat or skin on a dog's neck and, quite literally, shaking the dog. The severity of the shaking will depend on the size of the dog, the misdemeanour and the strength or determination of the handler. A handler should always know how best to deal with his own dog and quite often a young, insubordinate pack member will accept such minor physical contact as a way of admonishment. However, if a dog is showing aggression when its owner is present or towards its owner then such physical contact may result in the owner's being bitten. This is when common sense and natural instincts should preside. No matter how much other people may tell you what worked on their dog nor how much they try to convince you that being physical or 'scruffing' is the way to go, they are not the ones dealing with your dog. Neither should you encourage anyone to 'sort out' your dog, for, at the end of the day, it is you it must respect. If you are not in control of your dog and you are not the pack leader – and if it is aggressive then you are not – your dog will believe it is superior to you. As such it is within its rights, according to its instincts, to retaliate to any aggression you may show towards it. Remember: no confrontation with an aggressive dog; all it will do is frighten a nervous dog and antagonise a dominant one.

Outside the fight and flight distance the least dominant animal (canine or human) can retreat; inside the distance there is no retreat. If two dogs remain inside the fight distance they will make physical contact and the loser will be flat on the floor and the victor upstanding. To get to the winner–loser stage they will have been engaged in physical combat with teeth flashing and probably blood drawn; they will try to lock their teeth into each other's most vulnerable areas, the genitals or the neck. If we try to emulate this behaviour to become top dog we end up 'scruffing' the dog in order to prove that we are the dominant one. But are we? The simple reason that we emulate the dog's attacking the neck and not the other vulnerable area is that human beings unwittingly admit that they are different from the dog when it comes to confrontation. Now we are not looking so powerful when it comes to trying to 'beat them at their own game' are we? Why try to do something which, if it fails, will jeopardise our leadership potential and may place us at risk physically?

A pack leader rules quietly and therein lies his power, which, in turn, earns respect. Once a human being resorts to shouting and physical contact he is relegating himself to 'pack member' in status; he has shown a weakness

A big dog who is calm and relaxed.

in leadership and is noisily expressing a desire to join in the mayhem rather than to control it. The 'the loser will be flat on the floor and the victor upstanding', so omit the potentially dangerous middle part and put your dog straight on to the floor, quietly.

HOW TO SHOW LEADERSHIP PHYSICALLY

Back to my favourite words – common sense and instinct; always try to allow your gut instincts to come to the fore when you are striving to 'think dog'. We are not dogs and our dogs are not human; some of the pack rules can never be applicable and some may need to be tailored to fit our human ability to deliver. But the basic principle of the pack is the foundation for understanding the dog's mind and therefore it will assist us to communicate with our dogs, even the aggressive ones.

Let us look at the pack rules so far: the leader is in front at all times of uncertainty or possible danger. The leader makes it clear that the pack can relax within the pack area when he designates that it is safe to do so. The leader makes it quite clear that at any sign of a possible threat to the pack the members must assemble immediately behind him. If we now collate this information and 'read' it we can see that a dog showing aggression would begin to respect someone who stands in front in the leader position and, with quiet power, shows supremacy to an insubordinate.

If the 'down' command is operational then it is easy to put a dog on the floor, but it is rarely as easy to keep it there when it is striving to

We should never take a dog's mood or reactions for granted. This dog has changed from being relaxed to being predatorial in a matter of minutes. Not only has his body language changed but his eyes are more focused and harder. This is not breed related, any dog of any size can change this quickly, but it is often considered to be more threatening in a dog of this size than a smaller dog, yet a dog bite is a dog bite. For this dog giving him more space soon relaxed him again.

prove its importance. So lay the dog down and place your foot on the lead close to its collar, keep the hand loop of the lead in your hand and ignore the dog. If it struggles then tell it 'No'; when it is still and quiet give it a 'Good dog'. If this is done with the correct tones it works efficiently and with no risk of the owner's getting bitten. At no time put either your hand or your face near an aggressive dog. The mistake made by most owners is of being unable to resist the temptation to keep looking at the dog, shouting at it or stroking it when it is striving to get up. Remember subliminal training, tell the dog what it is doing and never give it a 'Good dog' when it is misbehaving; always make sure that you are between it and any threat.

DOES SIZE MATTER?

Before I close this chapter I would point out that when I use the word 'dog' I am referring to dogs in general; I do not have in my mind any particular breed or size. A large dog showing aggression is a formidable sight and, of course, carries a lot of strength. However, if anyone has ever been on the receiving end of a set of teeth belonging to a small dog which is determined to take the seat of your pants out he will know that the only difference size makes is strength and an overpowering vision. Aggression in a small dog can be every bit as nasty as that in a large dog, and if any dog thinks that it can

A classic show of fear in a dog but not submissive. The handler's body is relaxed and is placed between the dog and its fear, and is keeping walking forwards away from its fear and into a new space.

get away with being aggressive it is a potential danger. That sweet little dog that yaps and snaps in what appears to adults to be a rather futile and almost comical manner can cause grievous harm to a small child. Never underestimate the power of a small dog and never assume that all large dogs are dominant.

Next we are going to look at how we can restore confidence. We need to build up the confidence of a dog with nervous aggression so that it trusts its owner as a pack leader and we need to build up the confidence in all those of you who are desperately trying to control a dog with dominant aggression. But first let us take a look at how Craig is doing.

Craig's Progress

Three days of being served fresh food and water without eye contact and without giving him any reverence and I began to see the real dog behind the arrogant attitude he displayed. He sat in his pen, watching me, with one ear cocked and an inquisitive eye. His body language was beginning to show what he would like. He wanted to get to know more about me, but he was not inclined toward aggression with me; I had not challenged him and, more importantly, because I remained quiet and unconcerned, he was not sure how

strong I was. If a dog is given the opportunity it will think before it acts and Craig was not going to make the mistake of challenging someone who might be much stronger than he. There were only the two of us in this game of rehabilitation and, if I had any doubts about Craig, I was the only one to know them, and I was certainly keeping the fact a secret from him. As far as he was concerned I was an unknown quantity and, as such, he was showing me the respect of distance between us.

When I let him out of his pen into the building he kept a sensible distance from me while viewing his surroundings; he kept out of my space and I out of his. A light line had been left on him and, with his pen cleaned, I approached his side (never approach a strange or aggressive dog from the front since this places you in a threateningly confrontational position), picked up the line and walked out of the building. Craig had no option but to follow me; but when he passed me I turned and put him back in the pen. Two or three reruns of this and Craig followed me out of the building, and then waited, expecting me to go back inside. He was told that he was a good lad and we carried on across the yard; when he passed me he was taken back again. Craig had not yet been taught that, when told to sit or stay, he should do it without question so that I could not use this method to make him walk behind me. I could not begin to teach this until I knew that I had his respect as his pack leader and that he would not show aggression toward me. But I could not and would not allow him to take control outside by walking in front of me. The method I used was successful and, as soon as he understood that we did not go anywhere unless it was on my terms, I could begin the recall.

At this point I must also make it clear that on day one Craig had a complete change of diet. He had been on a high-energy diet from being a puppy and this had to be changed; he not only did not need it, but the excessive energy it yielded had been channelled into making his previous owners' lives a nightmare. With me he was going to be on zero exercise until he understood who was in charge, and he needed to be sober enough to be able to think clearly about all I had to say to him.

In most cases it would not be practicable nor even possible for someone with an aggressive dog to do as I did with Craig. The kennel, building and secure training area will not always be available, but neither will many owners be faced with a dog as formidable as Craig was. Hence the reason for using his progress to enable you to see how, by using methods a dog both understands and expects, they will actually help to form an alliance between owner and dog. Most of the problems associated with aggression were to be found in Craig, so by studying how I appealed to his pack instinct by the use of body language it will help you to sift out the information you can apply to your own dog in your own circumstances.

CHAPTER SUMMARY

There are two main kinds of aggression: nervous or dominant. Any other type, such as of possession or jealousy, will derive from one of these.

To be able to discover the reason for your dog's aggression and to understand it you must first learn to 'read' his body language so that you may communicate with him.

It is not necessary for a dog to be watching you in order for him to pay you attention, but it is necessary for him to be listening to you.

Never confront an aggressive dog and do not use physical admonishment; instead use your body language to tell the dog that you are the undisputed pack leader.

CHAPTER 5

RESTORING CONFIDENCE

Aggression does not suddenly appear; sometimes it may seem as if it does but there will have been indications to show how the dog or puppy will have been gathering the information which leads it to believe that aggression is acceptable behaviour. There is no miracle cure for aggression and it is often more difficult for the owner of the

If a dog is feeling vulnerable and there is not enough room to provide space you can make a dog feel secure by using something as a block. In this case a dog feeling vulnerable has a chair placed in front of him. With his back protected by the wall and his front protected by the chair he relaxes and lies down. Still watchful but feeling safer.

dog to address the problem than for an outsider. However, when a dog enters a different pack it will be a complete new beginning for it and, if the new pack leader makes the rules clear, then the dog will be more respectful of this person in a few short hours than it was of its owner. If the rehabilitation of the dog is successful it may go back to its owner prepared to abide by the new regime; but the success of this will depend on the owner's being educated in how to control the dog and then having the confidence to put it into practice. Education of the owner is essential, for either he is partly responsible for the dog's believing that it can make its own rules, or he has been unable to address the problems someone else has created. So the aim of any owner of a problem dog should be to learn how to re-educate their dog and to redress the balance from unruly or aggressive dog themselves to a well-mannered, pack (family) member.

NERVOUS AGGRESSION

The reasons for the nervousness are usually associated with a feeling of isolation; the dog believes that it is on its own without the security of a pack. The first thing you need to do is to reassure your dog that you are capable of protecting it, but this will not be conveyed if you are constantly stroking it, talking to it in a soft voice or giving it titbits.

First of all let us look at a dog that, from puppyhood showed signs of nervousness: where and when did the breakdown in communication begin? A puppy leaves the security of its mother and, without the advantage of education from senior canine pack members, it moves to a human home. It now needs to see familiar signs and messages; it needs a place of its own to feel secure in, a bed or a cage; it needs clear pack rules of where it can soil, eat, play and who is the pack leader. If it receives this instruction it will look to the pack leader for more guidance and this will come in the form of what it can and cannot chew, when to play and when to listen. Then will come the

lesson of keeping within the pack area when out on a walk and, of course, to come back when it is called. Recall will not be a problem if the puppy feels secure since it will want to be with its owner and not half a mile away from him.

Now take a puppy that leaves its mother and has no bed provided for it; it has to shoulder the responsibility of finding somewhere to sleep and feel safe. Or a puppy that has a bed provided but whose owner allows it to choose 'extra accommodation'. In both these instances we see a puppy making its own decisions; this immediately conveys the message that there is no leader and, whereas a dominant puppy will take over, a quiet, introvert one will be left wondering who is going to protect him. This is the first possible breakdown in communication.

The puppy that is passed to everyone for a cuddle could be a well socialised one, but it could also be made a nervous wreck. For if it is suffering from the effects of the problems described in the previous paragraph it has no leader and is being made vulnerable to everyone it sees. A pack leader would see that it was nervous and protect it, but if instead the owner continues to encourage people to handle the pup he is letting it down and destroying any chance he himself had of being a respected or strong leader. The time for a puppy to be socialised is only when it knows, trusts and respects its owner and there is no set time limit for this; it should be an enjoyable learning curve for the puppy, so nurture it.

When the pup goes for a walk it will expect its leader to keep it within the pack area. This can be measured quite easily by the distance that a dog could hear you at, were you whispering, no further than 20yd. But when the owner does not keep the pup within this area and, in fact, in most cases encourages it to go further for the sake of exercise then the last remnants of leadership are fast diminishing. So we are now looking at a puppy that has made its own decisions within the pack area, no one has told it how it should behave in a canine manner and the human rules are not understood because there is no common language. It is on its own, you are part of its pack, but it is really far too immature to be a leader and, when things go wrong, it is going to turn and run. If there is nowhere to run to it must stand and make as much noise as it can in order to appear strong.

These descriptions could fit a large breed of dog or a tiny lap dog, the only difference between the two is that the smaller dog will be picked up and this will offer some protection, but the large breeds do not get picked up as readily and are often expected to be brave.

The Older Dog

This may be a rescue or the puppy who is now older and beginning to show the problems associated with lack of leadership. The classic signs of nervous aggression are snapping, barking or growling at a dog or a person before it or he approaches its personal space, cowering and hiding either behind the owner or a fixed object. The tail will be between the legs and the general attitude will be to make a noise, sound vicious but nip and run. These dogs are often made worse when their owners try varying methods of training on them; these may serve only to add more instability to the already nervous dog. Listen to what your dog is saying, not the rest of the world, and supply it with what it needs: security.

TURNING NERVES INTO CONFIDENCE

Now is the time to take a look at what we have learnt about the pack and to use it to tell the nervous dog that it can rely on you. To begin

Dogs should always feel safe in their own place and they will often guard it. Even a small dog can become an aggressor and jump out at another dog, or person, passing the car. This dog is secured to make sure that cannot happen but there is also the threat to the dog of someone, or another dog, leaning into the dog's space. Never leave a dog unattended where he can be vulnerable or make a wrong decision.

with, forget about taking it out into areas that make it nervous or aggressive, take away any 'crutches' such as titbits or toys, cancel any training classes and examine its diet. If the dog is on high-energy food it could be exacerbating the problem by making it jumpy; nervous energy can also give a dog a feeling of false bravado, rather like a shot of alcohol. Your dog will also be on less exercise for a while so that its diet will need to be adjusted accordingly. Toys and titbits are not necessary, but if circumstances demand the use of them, then let it be sparingly and with discretion. Some dogs will show aggression toward other dogs and some to people but as a dog-training class will contain both do not take your dog to one until it has every confidence in you to protect it.

Case History (I)

Tina is a German shepherd and suffered from nervous aggression. Her owner could not take her to the local shops without her cowering behind her legs and growling at everyone who passed. She had been told to take Tina to classes and once a week to sit on a bench outside the shops to get the dog 'used' to people. By the end of a month Tina was trying to bite anyone who came near her and, in a desperate attempt to quieten the dog, her owner had resorted to offering titbits in an effort to divert her attention. This was, of course, actually rewarding the dog for its aggression.

Poor Tina was nervous and needed a leader she could rely on, but her owner was forcing her into situations that made her even more nervous. Tina saw the dogs and people at the training class as a threat and to be made to sit outside the shops with total strangers passing by was possibly her worst nightmare. As Tina was beginning to blame her owner for not only allowing this to happen but for actually taking her into these situations nervous aggression towards her owner was imminent. Back to basics. Tina had no recall, in fact, she was rarely allowed off the lead for fear of her running away, she did not pull on a lead except to try and get back home and she did actually go

behind her owner. But if we read the messages correctly Tina was behind her owner through fear and not respect; she did not pull because she did not want to go and she should have run back to her owner not away from her.

So for at least two weeks both Tina and her owner stayed at home; they did basic exercises in learning good manners and no toys or treats were used, instead she learned to appreciate her owner's telling her how proud she was of her and she began to enjoy pleasing her owner. Tina also began to feel secure since she was no longer being forced into frightening situations and, with patient handling, her owner encouraged her to walk behind with pride and not with fear. During this training a recall was developed by attaching a long, light line to Tina's collar and making sure that she knew to come back first time at every time. In the house Tina was given a bed of her own in a safe place. Instead of being allowed to wander around the house all the time she was given certain areas to sit in for a short period in each room before being given the freedom of that room. This served to explain to Tina that the house belonged to her owner and that she had the freedom of it but with permission. By the end of two weeks Tina was able to go for a short walk where there were no threats, she was feeling much more confident and she was learning to trust her owner. She felt secure in the house now that she had been given to understand it belonged to her owner, who was now proving to be a responsible leader, able to provide and to enforce pack rules and capable of protecting her. It did not take long for Tina to learn that whenever she was unsure of anything her owner would call her behind and investigate the possible 'threat'. Tina gained more confidence, she no longer cowered or ran behind her owner in fear and she was happy to let her pack leader deal with any situation that might arise. Six months later and Tina was back in training classes and would visit the shops without cowering. She will never be happy in crowded areas but she will visit them to please her owner who, in turn, never asks for too much from her.

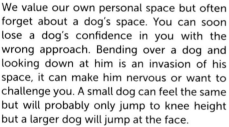

We value our own personal space but often forget about a dog's space. You can soon lose a dog's confidence in you with the wrong approach. Bending over a dog and looking down at him is an invasion of his space, it can make him nervous or want to challenge you. A small dog can feel the same but will probably only jump to knee height but a larger dog will jump at the face.

This is a kind and sensible approach to a dog. Sideways on and not bending directly over the dog. A gentle touch and the dog is free to move away if he wishes.

In Tina's case no titbits and no toys were used but in a similar case we did use a toy to help to keep the dog's mind off anything worrying it, but this was only in an emergency and it was employed to bring the owner into the game. Each time the toy had to be used the owner took the dog's attention from the object of fear, to the toy and then to himself, so the toy was used almost as a taxi for the dog's attention. After a week the word 'Listen', which had been applied each time the toy was used, broke the dog's concentration, making it look round and the owner then immediately took and held the dog's attention with voice and body language; after two weeks the toy was discarded.

Case History (II)

Megan is a Border collie, small, pricked-eared and very sensitive. Her owner lived alone in a large house and enjoyed Megan's company; her reason for contacting me was because Megan tried to bite her whenever she cleaned the house. Megan did not like the noise made by spray cans, she had 'complained' about polish and fresh air sprays to her owner by barking and yapping whenever they were used and had become so hysterical that she had actually jumped up and bitten her owner on the arm. This, of course, put a temporary halt to the cleaning and so Megan continued to employ the method of barking and nipping on cleaning days. Further investigation revealed that Megan pulled on a lead, did not always come back when she was called, most commands had to be repeated several times and on more than one occasion she had run away from her owner when she had heard a bang such as a car backfiring.

We employed similar methods as were used with Tina: toys and titbits were not a problem as Megan had never liked them. She had no bed and so was given a cage in order for her to have a 'safe house' when visitors arrived. In the cage was a small mattress, and when her owner wanted Megan to sit in another room or upstairs with her, she took the mattress. On cleaning days Megan was asked to sit on the mattress and was told to stay while the spray can was used. It took several weeks of training similar to Tina's to get to this stage, but Megan began to understand that the cage and the mattress were safe, that her owner could be trusted and was a reliable pack leader. Several weeks into training and Megan would sit while the spray cans were used; for a long time she needed to be prepared for the noise but each week saw an improvement. Out on a walk Megan was faced with the noise from pneumatic drills at some roadworks and she ran to her owner instead of away from her. She will always be an introverted little dog but she has learned security and happiness with her owner and therefore can face most of the things that each day offers.

Two dogs, both nervous and both, unwillingly, turning to aggression because they felt isolated. They had not received any clear messages about who was their pack leader, who to turn to for protection and neither of them felt secure in its house for, with no leader, there were no rules, no designated areas and no safe area. In many cases the larger the breed of dog the more isolated it can feel, for, although a large dog may be well equipped to look after itself as regards its strength, it still needs to understand the pack rules and to feel protected. A smaller dog may not be as strong nor as formidable looking as a large dog but for that very reason it often spends quite a lot of time sitting on knees and being held. This may not always be the best policy for teaching pack rules and it can often encourage insecurity, but the dog does not always feel the need to show aggression because the protection of its owner's body shields it.

The majority of dogs showing nervous aggression feel insecure when threatened by an outside influence, usually another dog or a human being. Once again we have to look at the basic rules for, if the dog is in front pulling on the lead, it is in control. There is a huge difference between a dog pulling or a dog walking in front, either on or off the lead, if it has been given permission to be in that position. A dog pulling is calling the shots since no leader worth his salt is going to allow a pack member to dictate where and when the pack moves. So the dog leads its owner down a path and sees an oncoming dog, what does it do? Its options are limited: stand and fight, but it is not very brave; turn and run, but it is on a lead; or run behind its owner for protection, but is the owner capable of protecting? In this situation the owner should have seen the 'threat' and called his own dog back into pack position before it began to feel threatened; this conveys the message to the dog that the situation is under control. If a dog feels threatened by another one and has no leader to rely on it will feel forced to make a stance, growling and snarling, not because it wants to fight but to try to protect itself against a fight. A dog will often appear to be more aggressive when it is on the lead because it does not have the freedom to move from the fight or flight distance. But a dog off the lead can pose a larger problem: without the restraint of a lead a dog can either run home (where are you as a leader?) or it can embroil itself in a fight; once this has happened you have lost even more credibility as a potential leader. Even if up to that point you actually had your dog's respect you should never, as a leader, allow your dog into a situation where it gets hurt: you are the protector and your dog protects you only when you are unable to look after yourself.

Case History (III)

Jack is a spaniel and, although he was not a nervous dog, he did not like other dogs near him. It is a mistake for owners to try to force their dogs to associate with others if they do not wish to do so. Jack was distraught at constantly being made to stand while other dogs were introduced into his 'space'; his owner was adamant that Jack had to accept the dogs they met on a walk but it was clear that his behaviour was beginning to turn to aggression. Jack's basic obedience was good, he did not pull on a lead and he both liked and respected his owner; however, he started to display a reluctance to go on his usual walks.

Jack's owner was showing a lack of respect for his feelings and had to learn to accept that Jack was an independent dog capable of choosing his own canine friends and should not be forced into what to him were intolerable situations.

Not all dogs are frightened of confrontation and not all want to fight and so it is essential that before trying to deal with any form of aggression the dog's attitude should be studied carefully and the underlying cause of the aggression thoroughly investigated. For this reason always be wary of the well-meaning person who gives you advice over the telephone without actually seeing the dog – this person is 'shopping in the dark', you are the only one

This dog is not happy about the approaching person, he has turned away but is on a lead so he has no escape route and his handler is not offering him any security.

who sees the dog all the time. If your dog is a rescue and you are not the one holding the key to unlock the door on all the 'silent reasons' the dog may have for its disturbed feelings you will be the interpreter of its actions, but you must learn to listen.

Case History (IV)

Chico is a cross-breed and, when his owner brought him to me, he jumped out of the back of the car and ran towards me growling. His owner made several mistakes in a row: she knew that Chico was nervous but did not restrain him in the car, instead she opened the door and allowed him to make his own decisions. Then, instead of commanding him in a firm but quiet voice, she screamed, this incited the dog into believing that she was backing him up. It is rather strange how animal instincts are still there in all of us, for my flight distance had gone but I had no wish to fight and so I stood my ground and quietly but very firmly told him to 'Stay'. There is no such thing as magic or of one person being better equipped to 'talk' to animals than another; all it takes is a little empathy and confidence. Chico did not instantly salute me or even take a liking to me, but he recognised by my manner that I was not going to back down and therefore it was possible that I could be more powerful than he. His owner was instructed to command him back into the car and then to stand in front of him; we now saw body language at its best. When Chico's owner stood at the side of him, leaving nothing between him and me (the threat) Chico snarled; when she moved in front of Chico but facing him he ceased to snarl but still growled; and when she stood in front of him and faced me Chico lay down. With the owner standing at his side, the dog was exposed to the threat; facing him, the owner was shielding the dog but leaving herself vulnerable; standing between the dog and the threat with her back to him meant that the dog was shielded and the owner (the pack leader) was in a position to be able to handle the situation.

Case History (V)

Barny is a terrier and had been left tied to his owner's car while his kennel mate was being trained. The distance between them was not great but it was enough for his owner to be unable to protect him when he was attacked by another dog. Although his owner ran to his assistance, he should never have left Barny in such a vulnerable position and he paid the penalty for his action. Barny lost all trust in his owner, hated going for walks and became terrified of other dogs. It took months of patience to convince this little dog that life was worth living and he never regained his confidence completely. If you think of all that we have learned about nervous dogs and leadership you will be able to work out yourself how Barny was re-educated. Dealing with aggression is serious but understanding dogs is fun; you have to be able to enjoy the good bits to help you to relax in the bad bits.

No two dogs and no two owners are alike and so it is important that each case of aggression is treated individually. For example, Breck was nervous of people and, when given a cage in the house for security, she began to use it as a crutch. She preferred to run to the cage rather than her owner and it appeared that by keeping her away from people she was beginning to grow content with her isolation. However, the fact that she preferred the cage to her owner served to impress upon us that she did not see her owner as protection and therefore the cage became a self-imposed prison rather than a safe house. Breck had to undergo periods when the cage door was closed, denying her access and she had to learn to rely on her owner for security in order to make it possible to take her out. This is another case of a dog which was naturally introvert and would never have been happy in any kind of competitive event, but as a companion she was ideal.

There are many ways in which nervous aggression can manifest itself, but if you study these case histories you will see that in all the cases the dogs were desperate for guidance

As the person gets nearer he has tried to move away but the lead prevents this, he is now displaying his fear with his lip licking and is still not getting any help.

Here we can see how to give the dog protection and to restore his confidence in his handler. As the person approaches his handler stands in front of him, her body language is strong but not dominant. Her hands are behind her back as a signal to him that all is well and he is looking up at her.

He is now feeling protected and has more confidence in his handler, and he peeps round her legs to have a look at the person approaching. He has the chance now to decide if he wants to interact with that person without feeling intimidated.

and protection, they needed a pack leader. There are times when teaching the basics may seem repetitive or uninteresting, but if you decided that you were going to buy a computer and intended to use it to its full potential it would be useless to you if you could not read nor write. You would be unable to operate the keyboard to be able to 'tell' it what to do and you would be unable to read whatever messages it displayed. If you do not learn to read and write in your dog's language you will never be able to communicate with it efficiently and this will often lead to a breakdown.

DOMINANT AGGRESSION

Puppies are not born aggressive, as they grow they will develop different characters and the interactions they share with each other will help to determine how and what roles they will play in the puppy pack. The puppy which appears to be the most dominant one in the litter is not necessarily a candidate for aggression when it matures, it is how this dominance is handled, or balanced, within either a dog or a human pack that determines the attitude of the mature dog. Similarly, the puppy which appears to be the quiet or introverted member of the litter is not necessarily destined to spend its life living on its nerves. However, if the first type of puppy develops aggressive tendencies it is more likely to be inclined towards dominance and the second type towards nervousness.

If a dominant puppy is allowed to make its own house rules and it is not made to understand that there is a leader to answer to, it will turn to aggression when its human cohabitants fail to deliver toys, games, food or any other requirements as and when it demands. Unlike the puppy leaving its mother that we studied under nervous aggression, this one will not feel isolated since he will enjoy making rules and giving orders.

When it comes to socializing a strong-natured puppy it must be made aware that at all times it must respond to its pack leader and without hesitation, or it will begin to play one person off against another. Within the family it will run to another family member, often with a toy or a ball, looking for a game and with outsiders it will endeavour to appeal to their affectionate nature, making its owner feel uncomfortable for calling it back. What may seem unimportant or even amusing in a puppy may be serious in a few short months when the pup is a dominant, arrogant adolescent.

The older dog cannot be 'retrained' until the reason for the aggression is determined; if it is a rescue then it probably arrived on your doorstep looking peaceful and within a week had begun to order you around. If you have had it from it being a pup then you will be able to cast your mind back to incidents that have encouraged your dog to believe that it is above you in rank, and you must be honest with yourself. If a dog shows aggression it will believe that it is within its rights to do so. It may simply be demanding your attention or it could be trying to attack another dog, but it will have believed that it is in charge and thus has every right to make the decision to act aggressively. The fact that it is not mature enough to make such decisions or that it prefers to behave in this manner first and then think afterwards or that you find it unacceptable is irrelevant. You either allowed it to develop within your pack or to enter your pack as the leader and so you do not really have grounds for an argument in his eyes.

Dogs need to feel safe and protected, if not they will make their own decisions. A dog that pulls on a lead is leading the way, and as the leader he will make decisions. If he sees another dog, or a person, he doesn't like he will make the decision of how to deal with them. Note the handler has his hands in front so when the dog pulls he will lose his balance, unless he goes faster to keep up with the dog.

REGAINING YOUR CONFIDENCE

You will soon lose confidence when a dog shows aggression: you lose it in your dog, your ability to control it and in yourself. You will begin to question your capability of ever being able to regain control and eventually you will find yourself resorting to any method available that deals with the moment but not the dog. Let me give you an example: your confidence is at an all-time low and you are nervous about taking your dog out for a walk in case you meet another dog and yours instigates a fight. But you still feel obliged to continue walking your dog; in fact, you can see no alternative because, of course, it needs exercise. In order to ensure that your dog cannot actually do any harm and to make you feel a little more confident in dealing with it you put a muzzle on it. This may work in that you may not be as nervous and therefore you are conveying a more confident attitude to your dog, but you have not changed your dog simply by placing a muzzle on him. You may have changed yourself slightly, but your dog will still have the same aggressive thoughts but cannot actually carry them out. He can, however, frighten another dog by his attitude; he can also pull you over and, if he is very dominant, he can even turn against you the next time you try to muzzle him. This same theory is applied to any form of appliance that makes your dog walk at your side: the dog is doing it because it has no choice, not out of respect, and, when there is a convenient lapse in your attention or the appliance is unavailable, the dog will revert to its bad manners. You do need to regain your confidence and you may need to use an aid to begin with, but try hard to manage without and, if you do need one, use it only as a means of primary education for your dog and not as a crutch that you yourself cannot manage without.

Training needs to be holistic; it is no good treating the symptom, you need to treat the cause. When you know that in certain situations your dog is going to react in a manner that you will find unnerving try to avoid those situations until such time as you are confident and able to deal with them. A dog showing aggression to other dogs in a group needs to be kept away from the group until you have made it quite clear to him that you will not tolerate his behaviour. You cannot explain anything to a dog when it is barking, growling and trying to fight every other dog in sight. How should you handle such a situation should it arise?

Let us first see whether your dog is obedient enough and has enough respect for you as a leader for you to be able to control him with body language. To begin with if your dog is threatening another dog then he is in control and will be in front of you, he will also be standing up and his body language will be stiff. What is your body language telling him? You will not be relaxed, in fact, you are probably as stiff as he is but for a different reason: his reason is he wants to attack but you are stiff with stress. You will undoubtedly shout at him and probably repeatedly, so your body language and the noise you are making will be as aggressive as his; this can serve to add to his already pumping adrenaline. Remember subliminal training? It is no good shouting 'No' to him when he is in full flight attack, for if he hears you at all he will probably only pick up the tone of panic in your voice. Should he hear the command and ignore it he is guilty of disobedience; if he hears it and does not understand it he will associate it with aggression. At this point you have lost control.

The dog's behaviour will not be a surprise to you; it will have shown aggressive tendencies before, so you should be cautious of any approaching dog. Before another dog comes anywhere near your dog's space you need to take action, and do not wait until your dog 'tells' you that it is going to be aggressive: you must tell it that you will not tolerate this behaviour. If you know that your dog is aggressive it should not be in front, you should be teaching it to walk behind and you should also be avoiding potentially 'aggressive' situations.

Tell your dog to come behind you and make him lie down, place your body between your dog and the approaching one and face the approaching one but do not take your attention from your own dog. This is the hard part since you must be aware of your dog and what it is doing but you must not give it any reverence. To talk to it in a soft voice, stroke it or give it any acknowledgement that it may perceive as praise, then you are condoning its actions. It hears, 'Down', 'Stay', and then 'Good dog' only when it is quiet. Can you make your dog do this?

If you know that this is not possible then you must go back to basics, you must also accept responsibility for any breakdown in communication and you must take away from your dog any concessions it has been allowed. It must learn to earn them. If it is aggressive on a walk then it cannot go on one until it accepts your leadership and until you have regained your confidence. Your attitude, feelings and state of mind are more important than his; you must believe this in order to get the situation into perspective and for him to learn that he is not as important as he would like to think.

Going back to the basics and being conscientious in your delivery of them helps not only your dog but it assists in regaining your confidence. Your dog will probably react adversely to begin with, but your determination at this stage and your patience will hold you in good stead as you progress with your new regime. It must be a new regime in order for your dog to be able to comprehend that things are going to change. You cannot say 'This is how it was yesterday, but today I am changing the rules.' You have a problem with your dog and so it is already choosing what it listens to and what it discards; it is not going to listen to any form of human communication that it does not understand or that does not please it. You have to make your statements in capitals in his language.

Let us take a good look at your dog: does it pull, have no recall, have to be told several times to do something? Does it bark at visitors, run at the garden fence when people pass, chase bicycles and cars? Does it play with a ball, chew toys, have a 'tuggy' toy? Does it demand to go for a walk when you put on outdoor clothes, bark when it wants you to hurry up, jump about in the car? Do you have children, do they play with the dog, are there any other pets, are you frightened of your own dog? Has your dog got plenty of energy, free access to a garden, and plenty of opportunity to exercise?

How many of these have you answered 'yes' to? The chances are that you will have answered 'yes' to most of them and in many cases all. If you have not found one of them a problem then ask yourself how honest you have been. A dog pulling for only the first 10yd of a walk does not constitute a dog free from a problem; it simply means that it settles down when it wants and the recall should be instant every time. Jumping up at visitors and then behaving still constitutes a problem dog; if your dog is aggressive you will have behavioural problems that have culminated in aggression. If you have answered 'yes' to all of them do not worry, it simply means that you have been totally honest with yourself and are ready to begin to deal with the problems. I would expect all the answers to be 'yes' in the majority of cases of dominant aggression. If your dog is a rescue then you may have a few 'don't knows', but the dog will actually 'tell' you its past if you study it. If it is aggressive to people of one sex and wearing certain clothes it is 'telling' you that it has suffered at the hands of someone similar. If it constantly tries to pull on its lead with its teeth or tries to make you play a tugging game it is 'telling' you that this is part of its past. If you play this game just once you are making it a part of its future.

I would also expect your dog to have boundless energy; one of the first things to look at is exercise and food. You will feel obliged to give your dog plenty of exercise if it is always full of energy, but you will also be creating an athlete. Each time you take your dog for a walk and it commits any of the 'sins' of the bad-mannered dog then you are allowing it to dictate to you how it will behave. If it will not listen to you or take notice of you on a walk then it must not go on one. Take heed of a golden rule: whatever a dog will not do 10yd away do not ask it to do 20yd away; restrict your dog's exercise to the garden and short walks and tire it mentally with as much education as you have time to administer.

Make sure that you adjust the diet accordingly to one of low energy and do not listen to any complaints from your dog of lack of variety or taste. If it had not been aggressive it would not be on a strict regime. If it has committed the crime it will do the time and it is neither as big nor as strong as you; it may be a Yorkshire terrier or it may be a Rottweiler, but it is only a dog and you are taller and stronger, if you put your mind to it. It does not pay the rent nor the mortgage, it cannot drive the car, it is unable to buy its own food and, left to its own devices, would probably end up with the dog warden. So it should be grateful to you for persisting with it and not giving up on it. Do you feel better now? Always keep things in perspective, you may have caused your dog's aggression or you may not, but whatever the reason for it you have not deliberately set out to give your dog control of your pack. So now you are going to make amends for mistakes made by yourself or others and get your dog under your control and back into pack position.

MAKING DECISIONS

You have to decide on your new regime and then you have to explain it to your dog. Let us pretend that you have just had a really bad day with him, he may have shown aggression to a human being, to another dog, to you or just been an arrogant pain in the neck. Pour yourself a drink and sit where you cannot see him nor he you. Now make a list: he has to have a bed and he must use it, decide what you are going to do about his diet, put all his toys away and throw the bag of treats out. Now go back to your dog, put on his lead, take him into the room and tell him to lie down at your side. Do not negotiate, do not point to the floor and do not wait to see whether he wants to listen. Never push down a dog that is aggressive towards you; if you think you are going to lose the battle about lying down then tell him to stand. You can do this by holding his lead and making sure that he is not allowed to move. So far you have not attempted anything with your dog that you cannot succeed at. Now watch him carefully and, when he tires of standing and wants to lie down, make sure that you give him the command first. Put your foot on the lead near his collar and keep him there; if you feel you cannot keep him down for long then give him permission to stand before he does, and make sure that he stands still. Now allow him some freedom, but he is not to play and he is not to be a nuisance. If he insists on annoying you, take up the lead and make him stand again. I would be making the dog lie down each time since this is the position he needs to be in to understand his place. You are aiming to do this, but if you cannot make the 10yd mark do not attempt the 20yd mark. So keep making him stand for in this way you are in control.

This is just an example of how you can begin to do something constructive immediately and without going out on a walk or having actually to deal with the aggression. This is the start of you rebuilding your own confidence. You are more important than your dog and your feelings are at the top of the list of priorities, therefore he must take a back seat and wait until you are ready to move forward. Try to apply this both mentally and physically to your dog. You also need to ensure that the members of your family understand what you are doing and that they appreciate the importance of supporting you and applying the same techniques and commands that you decide to use. Rebuilding your confidence and asserting your position as pack leader is a huge step and you need all the support you can get, but it is your inner strength that you need to learn to draw on. When your dog decides to take matters into his own paws and tries to assert his authority you then need to be mentally strong enough to prove your leadership and wise enough to know how to do it. This will come from studying your dog as a being, as a friend and as a dog with a problem. If you try to fight the aggression you will end up by fighting your dog; instead see the aggression as a mask and try to look at the dog behind it and realise that it is just a dog.

Keep him away from anything that is confrontational; for example, stay away from walks, other dogs and situations that bring out the worst in your dog. You need to assert yourself as a leader and he needs to forget how he has been used to reacting and learn how to respect you and your wishes. Dogs have memories, certain situations, sights and smells will trigger one and induce an action that the dog associates with that memory. For example, the dog that attacks the door when the post is delivered will eventually begin to react each time there is a noise at the door. The noise will trigger off the memory of the fun it had in the morning and it will react accordingly, and it will not be disappointed for you will react in a way that acknowledges his actions. He has made an impression, he has been noticed. The pandemonium caused each time he creates a noise will wind him up and eventually he will begin to think that it is his duty to carry the act further and actually be aggressive toward the 'intruder'. This, in turn, will make you even more stressed, there will be more noise and suddenly you and the dog are involved in a full-scale argument. He is not worth the argument and you must not let him think that he is; he must be told to go to his bed and stay there until such time as he is prepared to listen to you and behave with respect in your house.

Case History (VI)

Titch is a Jack Russell and had been attacked by a much larger dog when on a particular path with his owner. Titch was not a coward, he had put up a good fight and then convinced himself that he was invincible; each time he went on that walk he began to bristle and growl as he approached the point where the fight had taken place. His owner would tighten the lead and try to talk in a reassuring voice, these two actions alone convinced him that there must be something about to happen. By the end of a week it was becoming impossible to take Titch out, he was reacting aggressively before he reached the danger spot and was threatening other dogs, his owner was nervous of him and walks were becoming a nightmare.

Titch had been let down by his owner; he should not have been in a vulnerable position, but, of course, we humans are not perfect and there are times when we just get it wrong. The best course of action would have been to treat him with a little tender, loving care after the fight and then carry on with the walk. Instead he was carried home, which was unnecessary, fussed over and then taken back on the same walk in the evening. By this time he was convinced that monsters were lurking waiting to attack him and, because his owner had made heavy going of the situation, it was to the front of the dog's mind. A brisk walk and a game would have put it into perspective much quicker. As it was, it took weeks to convince Titch that his owner was capable of protecting him, of making him stay behind and lie down when he thought he would be likely to attack another dog, and keeping him away from the walk associated with the memory until he understood who was in control.

Case History (VII)

Suzie is a Yorkie and a sheep worrier. I must admit that I found this hard to believe when her owners came to see me and she curled up on the knee of one of them and it appeared as if butter would not melt in her mouth. I was told that she was a good dog, always did as she was told and always came back – until she saw sheep. If she ignored her owners when she saw sheep she was actually doing what she wanted, so further questions proved that Suzie did not come back if she saw a rabbit, a ball or another dog, but, I was told, 'That isn't the problem, it's the sheep.' A dog refusing to come back is an accident waiting to happen; it was tough luck for the sheep – they were the 'accident', but it could have been much worse, the dog could have caused a road accident.

I still found it difficult to imagine just how much of a threat such a small dog could be until I saw her with my sheep and she was like a vampire. The sheep were saved only by the fact that she could not run very fast, but the damage she was capable of causing while they were running was enough even without the way she used her teeth mercilessly when one was cornered. During the time Suzie was enjoying herself and creating mayhem with my sheep her owners were standing at the corner of the field calling her and telling her she was naughty. Suzie had received little discipline during her young life, lead walking had not been a problem since she was usually in the car or being carried. She did not need to sit or to stay since she was usually on a knee. She did not need a dog bed since she slept on the sofa. Being small this did not seem to pose a problem, but, as I have said several times earlier, a dog is a dog, Suzie may have been small but she had big thoughts.

These problems were nipped in the bud by applying the basic training of good manners

This dog is starting its walk knowing who is in control, where to go and any other decisions will be made by the handler. This is a strong dog and her body stance indicates she would love to be in control. The handler's hands are behind her back and her body is strong but gentle. She is parenting the dog in a language it understands.

Once the dog is settled the handler's hands drop to her side and the dog steps forward to walk at her side.

This is a lovely way to walk. The dog is striding out and taking in all her surroundings, the handler is relaxed with no tension in her hands or on the lead. The dog knows decisions are not hers to be made but she also knows she is protected. The lovely thing about such a nice way to walk is that both dog and handler have confidence in each other.

and a light line to teach her not to ignore the recall. But Polly, a terrier, was not brought under control when she began chasing livestock and she eventually bit a child. Both these cases had happy endings, both of the dogs were taught to listen to their owners, to respect them, to accept them as leaders and to do as they were told immediately. Both had shown aggression and neither had caused too much damage, but if they had not been re-educated they may not be alive today. They were both small dogs but they both displayed the kind of aggression that proved their instincts were canine.

Case History (VIII)

Gina is a Labrador and at seven months began to be aggressive at mealtimes. She would growl when her food was put down and, if anyone went near her, she would snap at them. This behaviour continued for some time until she turned on the youngest member of the family, snapping and trying to take food from him.

No form of aggression is acceptable and, in the case of a young dog entering a home as a puppy, good manners should have been part of its education, particularly when children are involved. Gina's owners had made the mistake of allowing both child and dog to play together with little supervision. A dog must be made to see a child, irrespective of its age, as hierarchy to them: when a child tries unsuccessfully to make a dog sit and the parents find it amusing it is actually lowering the child to the status of litter mate with the dog. The child should be encouraged to administer some basic instruction to the dog and the parents must make sure that the dog does as the child asks. If a dog sees a child as a litter mate it is well within its canine rights to establish itself as the leader of the litter and as such can nip any insubordinate litter member. Gina was rarely free from the toddler following her around and so aggression began as a warning to all in the room to leave her alone while she ate. The effect was such that she was not only left alone but she cleared the room; instead of telling Gina that she was out of order, and at the same time respecting her need to eat in peace, the family left her alone until she had finished. The theory of leaving her to eat her meal was correct, but not because Gina ordered it and not in the kitchen. It was inevitable that Gina would eventually begin to steal food from the toddler, her litter mate.

It took quite a long time for the family to understand the importance of Gina being treated like a dog and not a second child. She had a box full of toys and she found it difficult to understand why she could not play with the toddler's toys. She was spoken to almost as if she were a child and, when she began to act like a spoilt child, she had been given her own way. The first change was to make sure that the toddler was not allowed to interfere with Gina; this was a dog not a teddy bear, and the dog bed was out of bounds too. Then came some in-house training where Gina was told where she could and could not go, when she could have free time and when she had to sit quietly and have thinking time. The process of the owners' claiming their house back from a spoiled and aggressive dog had begun. Outside, the toys were put away and Gina began some serious lessons in lead walking, coming back when she was told and keeping one ear constantly on her owner's wavelength. Zero tolerance was operational until Gina accepted that she was a pack member and at the bottom of the list when it came to importance, when she accepted that there was a leader, and she was not to try to negotiate, and when she had learned some manners.

Case History (IX)

Ben's problem was slightly similar to Gina's but, due to different circumstances, his owners were advised to be more lenient with him and to try to find a happy medium between being in control but not distressing the dog. Ben is a Border collie and a rescue and when we sorted out his problem he was seven years old. He

Learning how to read a dog's body language can give us a better understanding of our own dogs, but it can also help us to understand dogs we meet along the way. This dog is clearly worried, would you approach him from the front or the side, would you approach him at all?

had suffered very harsh treatment before finding a good home with his present owners. He was possessive with his food, preferring not to eat it straightaway, but growling at anyone who went near his dish. This did not cause any distress to his owners since they understood that he had certain 'hang-ups'; he never actually showed any aggression towards them and so they learned to live with his habits. The problem arose when there was a change of lifestyle, elderly parents were moving in and Ben's owners would be out at work all day. The dog's behaviour upset the parents as they became nervous of him, the owners could not put Ben out in a run during the day because he had arthritis and they were afraid that the obvious nervousness of the parents would actually encourage Ben to turn aggressive.

They had sought advice and had, on the strength of this, been giving Ben his food and then making him sit and wait while they took it away for a few seconds before allowing him another mouthful then repeating the exercise. Ben's possessiveness over his food had now turned to aggression. To try this method with him was probably the worst thing they could have done, although I must say that if someone kept taking my dinner away I would probably attack him or her with my fork.

Ben had problems: his owners had rescued him knowing this and they were desperate not to have to part with him. He was no trouble at any other time, he loved them to bits, never left their side on a walk and never went far enough away to need a recall, he just liked his food, and who knows whether he had not been teased mercilessly before he was rescued?

A plan of the kitchen revealed a free corner that had no furniture and was not on a direct route to a door. A little DIY by Ben's owners and a decorative but strong screen, long enough and high enough for Ben to stand behind and feel secure, was erected. Problem solved, Ben's food was put behind the screen and no one had any need to go near it. When the new residents went into the kitchen they had no need even to acknowledge Ben; in fact, I advised them to ignore him completely.

Success! Ben began to relax when he realised that no one was interested in either him or his food, and the owner's parents ceased to be nervous of him when it became obvious that he was not meaning them any harm. It took some time but eventually Ben became far more trusting at mealtimes and stopped being possessive about his food. There are times when you need to compromise with a dog which is not being arrogant or dominant; Ben was just a mixed-up dog with a past and he needed a little patience.

Case History (X)

Rory is cross-bred and, when his owner brought him to me, he was excelling at agility, he loved competing and appeared to have unlimited energy. Rory's problem, or rather his owner's, was his almost manic excitement when he was competing and this had resulted in his jumping up and biting her arm on more than one occasion. Rory's diet was far too high in energy, he was a naturally energetic dog and did not need an extra supply; but the main problem was in his initial training. Rory's owner had used toys when she had begun preparing him for training, toys had later been substituted with the dog lead and, while preparing him for his competitive round, she had encouraged him to jump up, tug and pull at the lead. This brought Rory's instinct to grip with his teeth to the front of his mind and, as soon as he became excited or his owner's arm began to rise in the air, he jumped up and almost appeared to be attacking her. Rory had been taught to do this; it may have been a lead that was used to gain his attention and excite him but in the heat of the moment he was not going to stop and try to work out the finer points of what to attack. He was excited, his owner was excited, there was the noise of both humans and dogs close by, and he did what he had been educated to do, he just did not do it in the way that his owner wanted. Unfortunately, when his owner showed distress at his actions he became dominant. He could have taken a dislike to agility, blaming the sport

This dog is much more settled and almost welcoming to people but sometimes a smell or action can cause a memory trigger in a dog that makes it react out of character. No matter how friendly a dog seems we can't take it for granted that it will like us.

rather than his actions for his owner's sudden lack of enthusiasm for his prowess. This would have meant he at least respected her and wanted to please her, instead he became aggressive towards her and not just her arm.

I noticed that Rory chose to stand between his owner and me when we spoke, and when I moved he sat directly in front of her. I asked her to step in front of her dog but not to speak to him; Rory would not allow her to take the lead position, he kept moving in front, actually vying for leadership. You will by now, I hope, see the mistakes and will be thinking that Rory needed to be bought back into pack position and made to lie down.

Case History (XI)

Rex is a large dog and had the run of the garden. Because he had the freedom to go where he chose and to do as he wished in the garden he took possession of it. In his mind he was within his rights to take objection to people passing the gate and, when his furious barking did not deter passers-by, he began showing his teeth and threatening them. No one stopped this behaviour until he tried to bite a visitor; fortunately there was no harm done to the visitor but, of course, Rex was now classed as an aggressive dog. Would you consider him aggressive or had he been allowed to believe he was aggressive? If action had been taken earlier the dog could have been re-educated before he discovered the power to frighten people, first with noise and then with his teeth. If he had been provided with a place of his own in the garden, but not given the freedom of all of it, he would not have owned the boundary of the garden and therefore would not have challenged the people passing. The re-education process was a long one, first the garden was out of bounds without permission and then the area near the boundary had to be established as a dog-free zone. A pen was erected that Rex could call his own and he had to go back to the basics of training both in the house, where he had been doing as he pleased, and out on a walk. There will probably be a time when Rex forgets his new regime when an incident, such as a surprise visitor, will trigger a memory and he will display bad manners. If this happens his owners will be more aware of his thoughts and will be able to intercept them quietly and efficiently, as a good pack leader should deal with a bad-mannered pack member.

No more case histories, but we shall look at the Rottweiler being walked down a narrow lane by its owner, a quiet, well-mannered dog that was made apprehensive by the body language of a person approaching. The dog responded with a show of nerves, this induced what to the dog appeared to be an almost aggressive attitude from the 'threat'. The dog's owner immediately called the dog behind, the 'threat' relaxed his body language, the dog also relaxed and the walk continued without mishap and without a negative thought being planted in the dog's mind.

Never be tempted to run before you can walk; if your dog believes that he can dominate you his mind will not be changed overnight, so there is no need to rush things. Take some deep breaths, take stock of the situation and plan a course of action. But you must always be aware of your limitations, never try to do something with your dog that you think you are going to fail at. For you will pass this negative information to your dog and your weakness will become his strength. Aim to turn it around and make your determination your strength and through this you will weaken your dog's desire for dominance. Now let us see how Craig is doing.

Craig's Progress

Many weeks down the line with Craig's training saw him sitting, waiting, walking behind and recalling when told to do so. He had spent over a year of his life being aggressive and he was not going to change overnight, neither was he a perfect student. He knew that he had to walk behind, but he argued about it almost every day; the more he protested the more I made him walk behind. When he did as I asked without argument he was rewarded with freedom of the space in front of me. But in his favour if he saw anything that he felt aggression towards he automatically went behind me almost as if to say 'I feel like being naughty so I'll remove myself from temptation.' His recall, the command I consider to be extremely important, was good. In fact, on one occasion I was in the field and saw a black dog about to climb the wall on to the moors where over a hundred sheep were grazing; Craig had managed to open his pen door and was going walkout. I called his name to get his attention, then I gave him his recall and he came running back with a grin on his face and gave me a great big hug, while I stood with knees shaking like jellies. Craig's coming back was not a marvellous achievement, it was not the result of special or technical training methods and it was not because I have a unique ability to communicate with animals. It was because I stuck to my intentions of zero tolerance until I was respected – concessions must be earned, to my commitment to being the pack leader, to being patient and to liking the dog. You have to like a dog to be able to do anything with him and, despite Craig's arrogance, he never did *anything to give me a reason to do anything but like him. The methods I used may not always be possible for owners and hopefully you will not be dealing with a dog quite so volatile as Craig, but the mental attitude, determination and the ability to communicate with a dog are there within all of you. You are all capable of being a strong leader, but you have to believe in yourself or you cannot expect your dog to.*

CHAPTER SUMMARY

Confidence is important. A nervous dog needs to feel that it is not isolated. You must learn to be a pack leader who is capable of protecting it. A dominant dog will not feel isolated; it will enjoy taking control and you need confidence to be able to regain that control.

Be prepared to introduce a new regime both for yourself and your dog, and make it clear that if it wants concessions it must earn them. Applying rules and making the dog work to gain your respect will make it respect you. It will also give a nervous dog stability and a dominant dog boundaries.

CHAPTER 6

RECOGNISING YOUR CAPABILITIES

So do you understand the dog behind the aggressive mask a little better? Remember what I said about it being important to like your dog; it may sound a little presumptuous to suggest that you may not, but it is not an unusual situation. Craig's owners loved him greatly but they did not like what he had become, they did not like the idea of parting with him but they knew that they would never be confident enough to be able to handle him. They were also aware that he had been in control of them for too long; he was not likely to change his attitude to them and so he had to have a change of pack.

For a long time Craig was denied any ball games since he had been aggressive with his previous owners when they played with him. In this picture we are almost mimicking each other with our body language: I am asking the question, 'Do I have a ball for you?' His reply with his body is 'I don't know, have you?'

He has succeeded in climbing gently up, discovered that I have hidden the ball and is trying to open my hands. All my movements are smooth and calm, but notice how as he moves forward into my space it is a natural movement for me to move my head back out of his space. Now imagine an aggressive dog and a stranger in this invasion of space – the human would be tense and make a sudden move accompanied by a noise and the dog would attack, not the person so much as the situation created by him.

They still loved him, but they really did not like him very much. I remember once taking a dog for training and telling its owner how much I liked it; he commented on the fact that I rarely bonded with short-coated, hyperactive dogs like his, so it must be a good dog. It was a good dog and its character was such that I got on really well with it and liked it, but I doubt whether I would have grown to love it like my own dogs as it just was not my type of dog. This is no different from people I know: some I like and some I dislike, but I do not necessarily love or hate any of them. So ask yourself, do you like your dog – we know you love it, but do you like it?

SELF-ASSESSMENT

Are you a determined person or are you inclined to think that you are not capable of achieving what you want with your dog? You must be single-minded, if the seeds of doubt are sown in your mind you will transmit the fact to your dog. Are you frightened of your dog? If your dog is nervous you should be able to allay any fear of it when you realise that it is probably more scared than you are; in fact, it may even be scared of you. If your dog is dominant and you are frightened of it then I would advise you to think seriously of your capabilities before you try to demote it into pack position. It is a great responsibility taking a dog into your life. If somewhere along the way there is a breakdown in communication then the task of re-establishing communication and rebuilding the partnership becomes more onerous than ordinary training. When the dog assumes the role of a leader with nervous aggression it is not by nature confrontational, it is not wanting to show aggression, it feels that it has no choice. When a dog assumes leadership with dominant aggression it is quite prepared to fight. If you feel that you do not have the confidence to assert a show of mental strength to this dog or that you are not capable physically of keeping it in its place, making it keep behind, lie down and so on, then your priority must be for the dog's welfare and the safety of yourself and anyone else who may be involved.

I never encourage anyone to part with their dog without first giving serious thought to the consequences of where the dog will go and what will happen to it. But there are times when a dog needs to enter a new pack in order to make a fresh start. If this is to happen then prepare the dog as much as possible by beginning the process of demotion without entering a confrontation. You can address the diet, you can begin in-house training, and you can get him used to the idea of having to earn concessions. Very few dogs need to be destroyed owing to aggression, but it is a sad fact that many are, partly because, after a dog has bitten someone there is usually at least one recommendation that the dog should be destroyed. But if the owner cannot rehabilitate the dog then someone needs to be found who can and is prepared to do so. I have also spoken to people who have felt overwhelmed at the prospect of trying to gain control of a dominant dog. I have asked them to prepare it to be rehomed and, as the pressure of commitment lifted, within a couple of weeks, because they were not struggling to understand the dog out of necessity, they suddenly found themselves able to connect with its

Dogs that like to guard can even be protective over their water.

I believe that once a dog feels it needs to guard its food then I will leave it alone. I don't believe in taking a dog's food away from it, I wouldn't let anyone take mine! It's better to feed them out of the way in a quiet place and only move the dish when they have left it. Once a dog realises you are not going to take its food, it usually gets less protective. It's better to work on building up a good relationship than risk ruining it for something that isn't so important – unless you make it so – and it can right itself in time. It's better to have your dog respect you than feel it wants to fight you.

instincts and were able to keep it and retrain it themselves. This tells us a lot about how important our state of mind and confidence are when communicating with our dogs.

KNOW YOUR LIMITATIONS

There is no law that says you must proceed at a certain pace, and there is no one better equipped to know how fast you can proceed than yourself. Decide how you think that you should go, listen to advice but do not be pushed into anything that you are not prepared for. If you have a small dog you will find it quite easy to handle it on a walk when it is trying to get in front of you, but a large one may pose a problem. Always keep one

step in front mentally and physically; once a large dog gets in front it has all its strength to pull against your outstretched arm. Endeavour to keep it behind when you have all your strength in your body and neither the lead nor your arm is being pulled.

Try to look for any pitfalls since prevention is better than cure. Stay away from any toy that makes a noise that can be associated with something else; for example, a ball that, when squeezed, emits a sound that could be mistaken for a child giggling or crying, and there are such toys. If a dog gets fun out of such a toy and is encouraged to play with it the consequences could be disastrous. Do not encourage your dog to chew its lead, in fact, discourage it from chewing anything. I have a saying with my pups, 'No teeth' and they soon

Some dogs actually like to look after their owner's belongings, this can be sweet as long as it doesn't turn to guarding. This dog is peacefully keeping an eye on the bag, the problem is it's by the door and if someone were to enter it could then turn to guarding.

Some big dogs are just softies and keep a patrol on the boundaries but aren't aggressive.

understand it. If I say 'No' they know that they must stop what they are doing, but 'No teeth' means that they can still carry a ball or play with whatever they have but they cannot use their teeth on it. Think about it, for it makes sense to explain to the dog what it can and cannot do.

Do not fall into the trap of having two puppies together. I have lost count of the times that I have had owners driven to distraction by two dogs that have bonded with each other to the exclusion of their owners as anything other than a caterer. Two dogs together of the same age will be able to communicate naturally with each other; they need senior canine supervision to prevent them becoming complacent. If you are not able to simulate this supervision then wait for at least a year before getting a second dog.

ACCEPT YOUR DOG'S LIMITATIONS

If your dog is dominantly aggressive towards other dogs then you may have to learn to live with it. Some dogs will accept full rehabilitation, others will always hate dogs of their own

Some dogs love all people but just won't tolerate other dogs.

sex. This does not mean that you do not attempt to rehabilitate or to improve the situation; learning to live with it is not the same as simply accepting it. Your dog must learn that it might have a natural hatred of something but it cannot make the rules in your pack. A long-term rescue of mine hated other senior males; he was lovely with bitches and youngsters but a fight waiting to explode when he saw a senior male. I took responsibility for the dog and I accepted that he was always going to pose a problem in this regard; it meant I had to be diligent when I took him out. On a lead he was taught to ignore other dogs; if he was loose and saw another dog he would come back to me without an argument. However, any excuse was a good one to have a scuffle and, if someone shouted or panicked, he would dive in first and ask questions later. I always had to be in a very calm mood if we were faced with a volatile situation.

Socialisation may actually do some harm if your dog does not understand that you two are a unit. A dog that is encouraged to go and meet other dogs and to socialise with them is not developing one of the natural instincts it needs. The impression that all dogs are friendly and will welcome its advances can cause serious trouble if it approaches a dog that does not take kindly to strangers. The second dog is

Some dogs don't mind either other dogs or people but really don't like being fussed.

using its natural instinct; the first one does not understand canine law. But it is a dog and if it is not allowed to develop as one then what is its position in life? Our job is to nurture the instincts and balance them in order to produce a confident dog, not to take them away and leave it without its natural culture. My records are full of dogs of about twelve months in age suffering from aggression after being attacked when jumping all over a strange dog when out on a walk. The dogs are aggressive, they have lost faith in their owners and they are not sure how to behave because they are not human and have not been taught 'dog'.

AVOID HYSTERIA

Some of the things that may seem amusing in a puppy can be potentially dangerous as the dog matures. Chasing in any form is a prelude to hysteria – cats, cars, bicycles, birds, and before long it will be rabbits, sheep, children; when we get to the last one it is often too late. Barking at the television and biting the screen: I have a dog who watches football, but he watches it, he does not turn into a thug trying to smash the set because no one will let him play with the ball.

If your dog shows aggression towards other dogs or people you are not in control, but if your dog thinks that you are so low down in the pecking order that it can bite you, then the problem is far more serious. Not irreparable, but do not expect it to be an easy road to recovery. One of my dogs has done a lot of television work and can be taught to do most things, but when I tried to teach him to jump up and pretend to bite my arm for a video, he was horrified. It caused him so much distress that in the end we cut the scene; there was no way in which he was going even to pretend to bite his 'mum'.

LENIENCY

There are times when rules do not have to be kept to all the time; I call it living in the grey area. But before a dog can enter a grey area

What we are all striving for is a happy dog that trusts us, feels safe with us and it knows we are not going to pressure it to be anything other than itself.

it must first be fully aware of the 'black you can't do' and the 'white you can do' areas. Dog training begins with the black and the white and the more this is impressed upon a dog the sooner it can live in the grey area; but an aggressive dog cannot enter a grey area until it has understood and accepted all your rules. You can exercise leniency only when you fully understand your dog. Two of mine rarely walk behind me; they will willingly do so should the situation demand it, but most of the time they are within a few feet of me, happily going about their business and always listening to me. If a 'threat' were to appear in front of us they would automatically come behind; but another of my dogs has to keep being reminded that his place is in the pack, not leading it. He is a dominant dog and would love to be able to sort out any potential 'situation'. The first two would be candidates for nervous aggression, but the third one would be dominant aggression; none are aggressive, but neither are they handled in the same way nor do they have the same concessions. All dogs are individuals and the mistake we often make is to categorise them as dogs rather than introduce them into our lives as individuals, but we do need to keep in mind what they are. If we want to teach them human ways we must first familiarise them with their own culture.

CHILDREN

Dogs and children can mix and they can learn a lot from one another, but to allow them to mix without supervision is a mistake. Dogs will soon see children as litter mates and will begin to boss them around. But a dog does need protection from children; no dog should be subjected to being a surrogate toy and every dog should have a place of its own that is a child-free zone. If it is too difficult for someone to teach children that the dog bed is a no-go area then I question their ability to be able to teach the dog anything. It may sound harsh but better a harsh word now than a bitten child and a dead dog later; dogs do not ask for

much and they are entitled to a place of their own and some privacy. Children love responsibility, so rather than encouraging them to play endless ball games with the dog, educate them in the elements of responsible dog ownership. Children are never too young to learn, and, if they are, then they are too young to be alone with the dog.

We have covered only the basics of training; we are dealing with aggression and to confuse this with anything other than the foundation commands for good manners would have sidetracked us. If your dog is aggressive no amount of training will help if you do not put in this foundation. I cannot stress enough the importance of the 'big four': you will walk behind, stop, stay and come back every time and at the first time of asking and I will not negotiate. Any dog educated to these simple rules from day one will not pose a problem; unfortunately, we tend to allow a settling-in period before starting the education, and by that time the dog has usually written its own script. In addition to the first four commands here are four more for you: I will be committed to a new regime, I will reinstate myself as pack leader, I will not negotiate and I will spend time on in-house training and learning to 'think dog'. This last one is especially important: always ask yourself, 'What is the dog thinking?' It is far too easy to presume that you know what it is thinking and what its reaction to certain situations will be, and then, with that presumption to decide how to handle it. But have you stopped to see whether the dog really did think what you expected it to, did it really act as you thought it would? If you assume that the dog will be nervous the first time it is in a car it probably will be, but if you put it in the car and watch for its reaction rather than assume what it will do, you will act on instinct no matter what it does. You will be allowing the dog to communicate with you rather than your 'telling' it to be nervous and, if it is unsure, you react to the moment. If you throw a ball and expect the dog to bring it back, you will be put out if it does not retrieve it and exasperated when it is difficult to

A handsome lad, isn't he? This little dance is another way of trying to persuade me to play with him.

At last, it's within his grasp! Look at our body language again: we are almost identical, both in a similar position, both relaxed and focused on each other. Despite the fact that Craig wanted to play, he wanted the interaction with me rather than the ball. For him this is his quality time, for me it is time out with a dog who has become a friend.

teach the command 'Fetch'. If you roll the ball towards the dog and allow it to decide how it wants to play with the ball the time will come when it brings it to you on its own accord; it will seek your interaction rather than you demanding to be included.

That is a little insight into how to think dog and thus begin to create an empathy between you. Inside that four-legged body, be it a large one or a small one, is a friend and if you can stay the course it will be worth it, but you must always remember that the outcome may not be what you originally had in mind. Once a dog has used aggression as a power tool it will always know the tool is there. If the tool

is never used the dog will be unaware of its existence, but no matter how successful you are at rehabilitating your dog it will always be lurking in the background and, if the balance is tipped, it may surface again.

A nervous dog may not be mentally equipped to compete in any sport; a dominant dog may be quite happy to compete but a liability for quite some time, if not indefinitely. If a dog shows aggression towards your partner he has no right to be protecting you when you do not need it, so jealousy is rearing its head. When you have solved the problem make sure that you do not have an argument or friendly scuffle when the dog is present since it may not be able to resist the temptation of using it as an excuse to have a nip, then you will be back to square one.

You must always be aware that, if the aggression was there, it will not have vanished; it may never be seen again but there is a better chance of that if you do not forget that it existed. You have to be confident that you are the leader and that you can control any situation that may arise; do not anticipate situations but do not dismiss the possibility of them arising either.

Above all, remember that there is a light at the end of the tunnel provided that you keep going forward and the nearer you get to that light the easier it becomes. The struggle at the beginning to get it all together, remember it all and learn to think dog may seem almost impossible, but every day you dedicate to commitment is a day on a learning curve for you as well as for your dog. As each week goes by you will begin to find it easier to think dog and you will derive immense satisfaction from being able to understand what he is trying to say to you. You are capable of running your own pack; if you had not been willing to try you would not have wanted to learn about aggression and so you are halfway there already. Have faith in your own capabilities and have faith in the dog behind the mask, for when you see a smile instead of a snarl you will also see respect and love, and you will have earned that.

What Happened to Craig?

Craig will spend the rest of his days with me, he is a very personable dog but I do know his limitations. He cannot be trusted with male dogs and he will certainly show aggression towards anyone entering his space if I am not present. However, to be fair to him, my time with him has been limited and if I could have concentrated on just him for a longer period he would be capable of much more now.

He has a good life, he has his own 'dog house' and can have female canine visitors for company. He loves bones and, yes, he will let me take any food, including his bones, from him, but I never do it unnecessarily; I would not like it, so why I should I do it to him? He enjoys his walks and he loves playing with a ball, although for a long time he was not allowed one. I keep all his games controlled; when a ball is thrown he has to wait for a minute before going for it, he brings it back quietly and, when told to 'Leave', he gives it to me. I always take care to let Craig know the situation before I do anything with him; if I remove his bone or take his ball I always warn him what I am doing and not to interfere. If I were not to do this and I took him by surprise I would only have myself to blame

if he growled at me; if this happened he would probably be horrified at what he had done, but he might also think that he could do it again. So no confrontation; it is not a hardship to tell the dog what I am about to do, in fact, it is good manners; I never just take things from any of my dogs, but with them it is out of courtesy, with Craig it is out of respect for his past.

Craig is with me because no one else would take him; I accepted the responsibility for him and he has a permanent home with me. I can honestly say that he has never turned a lip nor growled at me and he is never any trouble. His pictures tell his story and show how his attitude changed from aggression to warning. If someone is threatening his space he will warn them to keep away; if I tell him to be quiet he wags his tail. Craig knows the power his aggression has over anyone who is nervous and he thoroughly enjoys trying to exercise this power; in fact, I am sure that he derives a great deal of amusement from it. My situation allows me to keep Craig without any problems; in a domestic environment it would be more difficult, but as I have already said, few dogs in pet homes are as violent as Craig was.

Craig's progress has been monitored to help you to understand the possibilities and to explain how dogs have a natural concept of pack leadership. If you communicate in a way your dog understands you can use this instinct to show it that it is worthy of pack position, but that you are the pack leader. It is amazing how a slight movement of your body across the front of your dog can change his thoughts. Nearly all of Craig's initial rehabilitation had to be done with body language as he had no respect for the spoken word.

Craig has gone from being a dominant, aggressive dog with absolutely no respect for human beings into a good-looking, obedient, faithful dog. I will always have to be aware of Craig's 'space' and make sure both people and other dogs respect it, but as I am the main person to deal with him this does not pose a problem. As far as my relationship with Craig is concerned, he began his time with me by being curious, he has argued with me and he has tried to test my patience but now we are good friends. Craig's repayment to me is in the light in his eyes and the kiss he gives me when I put him to bed for the night. He has never been a bad lad, he was just allowed too much too soon.

Craig is now a happy, relaxed dog and a very handsome one. His eyes have lost the cold, hard stare and are now warm and friendly. He is no angel, he is full of fun, cheeky and mischievous, but he is well-mannered and enjoys a happy, normal life.

FINALLY

If your dog's story turns out to be half as satisfying as Craig's you may be proud of yourself, for you will have achieved what you set out to do. And, believe me, what you may lose by having to accept certain limitations you will gain in the knowledge that your dog sees you as a pack leader, the top dog and you cannot get a better compliment than that.

Epitaph

Craig passed away peacefully in 2009. He was at least fourteen years old and in the time we were together he changed from being an angry dog to one who loved life and was full of fun. He has left a legacy of knowledge and understanding that has helped so many dogs that have come into our rescue. Craig lives on in everything I learned from him.

RIP beautiful boy

Index

First published in 2001 by
The Crowood Press Ltd
Ramsbury, Marlborough
Wiltshire SN8 2HR

enquiries@crowood.com

www.crowood.com

New edition 2024

British Library Cataloguing-in-Publication Data
A catalogue record for this book is available from the British Library.

ISBN 978 0 7198 4365 5

Photographs by the author and M. Merone.

Typeset by Chennai Publishing Services

Cover design by Su Richards

Printed and bound in India by Parksons Graphics Pvt Ltd

RELATED TITLES

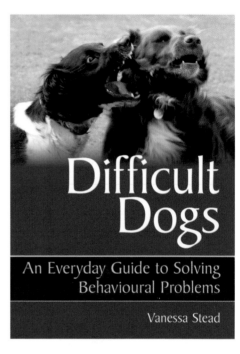

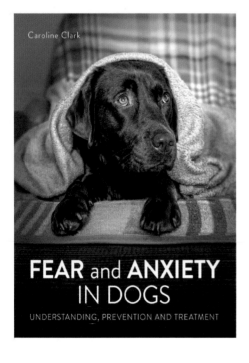

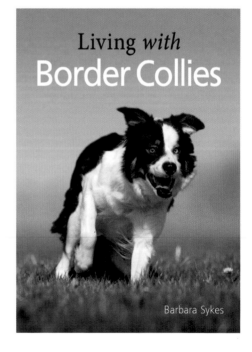